TO THE BRINK

JFK and the CUBAN MISSILE CRISIS

BY **Stacey Bredhoff**

With a message from

David S. Ferriero

Archivist of the
United States

TO THE BRINK
JFK and the Cuban Missile Crisis

By Stacey Bredhoff
With a Message from Archivist of the United States David S. Ferriero

Designed by Rania Hassan
Edited by Patty Reinert Mason and Benjamin Guterman

Copyright ©2012
The Foundation for the National Archives, Washington, DC

This book is based on the exhibition "To the Brink: JFK and the Cuban Missile Crisis," presented in the Lawrence F. O'Brien Gallery at the National Archives Building, Washington, DC, from October 12, 2012, through February 3, 2013, and at the John F. Kennedy Presidential Library and Museum in Boston, Massachusetts, from April 12, 2013, through November 11, 2013.

"To the Brink" was created by the National Archives and its John F. Kennedy Presidential Library and Museum and made possible in part by the Foundation for the National Archives, the John F. Kennedy Library Foundation, and the generous support of Lead Sponsor AT&T, with special recognition to the Lawrence F. O'Brien Family.

In addition to its support of this exhibition, AT&T assisted the National Archives in creating the nation's largest online digitized Presidential archive, providing unprecedented global access to the most important papers, records, photographs, and recordings of President Kennedy's administration.

For the Foundation for the National Archives
A'Lelia Bundles, Chair and President
Thora Colot, Executive Director
Patty Reinert Mason, Director of Publications
Kathleen Lietzau, Publications and Research Assistant

For the National Archives and Records Administration
James Gardner, Executive for Legislative Archives, Presidential Libraries, and Museum Services
Christina Rudy Smith, Director of Exhibits
Rania Hassan, Designer
Benjamin Guterman, Editor

For the John F. Kennedy Presidential Library and Museum
Tom Putnam, Director
Stacey Bredhoff, Curator
James Wagner, Exhibit Specialist

Library of Congress Control Number: 2012948241
ISBN: 978-0-9841033-8-6

First published in 2012 by the Foundation for the National Archives
700 Pennsylvania Avenue NW, Room G12, Washington, DC 20408
www.nara.gov/nae/support

Printed in the United States by Todd Allan Printing

Front cover: Customers in a California department store watch President Kennedy's televised address, October 22, 1962. (Detail; image adapted. *See page 40)* Photograph by Ralph Crane. ©*Time & Life Pictures/Getty Images.*

Back cover: Illustration of a target map depicting the potential range of nuclear missiles erected in Cuba by the Soviet Union in 1962. By Ray Ruskin.

Inside front cover: President Kennedy's address to the nation, October 22, 1962, page 1. *John F. Kennedy Presidential Library and Museum. Inside back cover:* Limited Nuclear Test Ban Treaty, August 5, 1963, page 1. *General Records of the U.S. Government, National Archives and Records Administration.*

CONTENTS

MESSAGE FROM THE ARCHIVIST

In the fall of 1962, as the United States and the Soviet Union stood at the precarious brink of thermonuclear war, President John F. Kennedy gathered around him his closest advisers to decide what to do about the Soviets' installation of nuclear missiles in Cuba—close enough to reach the United States in less than five minutes.

The exhibition, "To the Brink: JFK and the Cuban Missile Crisis," and this accompanying publication take us on a behind-the-scenes tour through the harrowing 13 days of the crisis. Through transcripts of White House recordings made by the President, as well as artifacts and original documents drawn mainly from the holdings of the National Archives' John F. Kennedy Presidential Library and Museum, we are able to follow the closed-door debates of the President's special advisory committee, the "Ex Comm," in real-time and to observe Kennedy's decision-making process as he navigates the crisis and crafts the U.S. response, averting all-out nuclear war.

Analog audio recordings are converted to digital formats at the John F. Kennedy Presidential Library and Museum. Bill Bjelf, Assistant Digital Archivist for Audiovisual Collections, works at the Kennedy Library's Digital Audio Workstation.

John F. Kennedy Presidential Library and Museum, Boston, Massachusetts [NLJFK2012-D11]

Unbeknownst to almost all of the participants in those meetings 50 years ago, JFK had previously asked a Secret Service agent to install a recording system at the White House, with reel-to-reel machines in the basement of the West Wing and microphones hidden inside his Oval Office and the Cabinet Room.

The taping system recorded nearly 250 hours of White House meetings, including most of the ones that took place during the Cuban Missile Crisis. Portions selected from the 43 hours of tape transcripts from the episode are included in this publication.

The President's purpose in creating the tapes remains unknown, but the recordings, recently digitized at the Kennedy Library and made available online, are now part of an incredible treasure of textual, photographic, and audio records that allow us a fuller and more immediate experience of this major event in our history.

To the Brink, one of four publications marking the 50th anniversary of the Kennedy administration, also draws on information that the major players in the crisis didn't know at the time, giving us the perspective gained over the past five decades as superpower tensions eased and participants reflected on how close they came to mutual destruction.

The records featured here—fascinating as they are—are but a small sample of the billions of records the National Archives holds in trust for the American people. These records include paper and parchment documents, audio and video recordings, motion picture film, photographs, maps, drawings, and electronic records.

At the National Archives, we are proud of the work we do to preserve the vital records of our nation and to make them accessible to the people, arming citizens with the tools they need to fulfill their role as watchdogs on our democracy.

Exhibitions like "To the Brink" and the publications that accompany them help us to introduce the records of the National Archives to new audiences around the globe.

I hope *To the Brink* will inspire you to visit us in Washington, in Boston, or at a National Archives facility or Presidential library closer to your home. These records are yours, and I invite you to explore!

David S. Ferriero

"The Communist empire . . . which knows only one party and one belief . . . suppresses free debate, and free elections, and free newspapers, and free books and free trade unions—and . . . builds a wall to keep truth a stranger and its own citizens prisoners.[1]

September 25, 1961

I think that anybody who looks at the fatality lists on atomic weapons, and realizes that the Communists have a completely twisted view of the United States, and that we don't comprehend them, that is what makes life in the sixties hazardous.[2]

December 17, 1962

President John F. Kennedy, October, 1962

Photograph by Cecil Stoughton

John F. Kennedy Presidential Library and Museum, Boston, Massachusetts [ST-464-22-62]

TO THE BRINK
JFK and the CUBAN MISSILE CRISIS

It was a close call—maybe the closest call in human history.

For two weeks in October 1962, the world teetered on the edge of thermonuclear war and the end of civilization as we know it. Earlier that fall, the Soviet Union, under orders from Premier Nikita Khrushchev, began secretly to deploy a nuclear strike force in Cuba, just 90 miles from the United States, with missiles that could reach most major U.S. cities in less than five minutes. President John F. Kennedy said the missiles would not be tolerated, and insisted on their removal. Khrushchev refused. The standoff nearly caused a nuclear exchange and is remembered in the United States as the Cuban Missile Crisis.

For 13 days, the fate of the world hung in the balance. For all his muscular, anti-communist rhetoric, the President's response was remarkably restrained. Under unimaginable pressure—as the Soviets raced to complete construction of the missile sites—the President refused to be rushed. He conducted the negotiations with discipline and delicacy, balancing cold resolve with pragmatic statesmanship. He would not accept the missiles, but neither would he force the hand of an impulsive opponent into a rash response. And on October 28, 1962, with the world's mightiest military forces bristling with anticipation, and events spinning out of control, Khrushchev suddenly relented. The missile sites, he announced, would be dismantled immediately. The peaceful resolution of the crisis is considered to be one of President Kennedy's greatest achievements.

To the Brink is a look back at the crisis from the 50-year mark. It is drawn mainly from U.S. sources and presents a U.S. viewpoint. Pieces of the story that appear hazy now may come into sharper focus over time; others that are now clear will blur as the episode recedes further into history. And perhaps the most intriguing questions of all, which concern the mystery of human behavior, will remain unanswered—known only to the men who looked into the abyss of a nuclear catastrophe, and then stepped back.

THE **BACK STORY**

The Cold War is the term for the rivalry between the two blocs of contending states that emerged following World War II. It was a series of confrontations and tests of wills between the non-Communist states, led by the United States and Great Britain, and the Communist bloc, led by the Soviet Union. It was this rivalry that, in October 1962, brought the world to the brink of thermonuclear war.

Nikita S. Khrushchev was Premier of the Soviet Union during the Cuban Missile Crisis. He came from a peasant background and—with little formal education—rose through the ranks of the Communist Party during the regime of Joseph Stalin, whose bloody purges claimed millions of lives. Khrushchev successfully conspired to succeed Stalin as Soviet leader after his death in 1953. Although Khrushchev introduced reforms and put a new face on the Communist Party, he relied on many of the same strong-arm tactics to retain power. In Cuba, Khrushchev saw an opportunity to gain a foothold for Marxism-Leninism in Latin America and thus strengthen the worldwide Communist movement.[3]

Nikita S. Khrushchev,
Moscow, U.S.S.R.
April 12, 1955

© Corbis

Suddenly poor little Pinya drew himself up and said, 'Comrades, you elected me by democratic process as your leader. There-fore, I will go first.'

"The moral of the story," Khrushchev explained, "is that no matter how humble a man's beginning, he achieves the stature of the office to which he is elected.

"That little Pinya," he concluded, "that's me."

It is not clear whether the tale was meant as a parable approximating actual events, but it did reveal much about Khrushchev's mental reflexes: his consciousness of his hum-ble origin, a frequently reiterated theme; his sense of per-sonal accomplishment; confidence that his vigor, initiative, and capacity are equal to his station; jealousy of the pre-rogatives of that station; and a wry satisfaction with the cunning which had enabled him to gain the upper hand over a series of rivals who underrated him.

When Stalin died in 1953, Khrushchev was largely an unknown quantity outside the Soviet Union, seemingly a lesser-ranking figure than the better-known Molotov, Malenkov, Beria and Mikoyan. In the year or so that ensued he edged his way more and more onto the public stage but the picture he presented to foreign observers was not impressive--from all appearances he was an impetuous, obtuse, rough-talking man, with something of the buffoon and a good deal of the tosspot in him.

- 2 -

Before long, however, events would show that there was a great deal more to Khrushchev than the appearance suggested and that behind the exterior lay a shrewd native intelligence, an agile mind, drive, ambition, and ruthlessness. His own colleagues probably sold him short initially, but they un-doubtedly knew from experience that he could not have escaped Stalin's murderous judgment if he had been witless or foolishly impulsive.

It now is clear that he had other qualities which had had only limited opportunity for expression under Stalin-- resourcefulness, audacity, a good sense of political timing and showmanship, and a touch of the gambler's instinct.

Humble Beginnings

Even without benefit of propaganda embroidery, the story of Khrushchev's rise to the Soviet pinnacle makes a model Communist success story. He was born in 1894 in the small village of Kalinovka, not far from where Great Russia meets the Ukraine, the son of a miner not long removed from the fields. His boyhood was spent in poverty and he recalls with pride that he worked successively as a shepherd and as a miner. He neither can nor wants to forget his humble be-ginnings and his speech is larded with peasant proverbs and even Biblical phrases which go back to that period. His

Fidel Castro, the illegitimate son of a wealthy sugar planter and a household servant, came to power in 1959, at age 32, after leading a rebel army that toppled the dictatorship of Fulgencio Batista. Subsequently, Castro consolidated power in his own hands, postponed the free elections and reforms promised by the revolution, cracked down on all political dissent, and eventually declared Cuba a socialist state. Thousands of Cubans were executed between 1959 and 1962; hundreds of thousands more fled the country.[4] Castro actively sought the economic support and military protection of the Soviet Union, openly aligned with its policies, and eventually became a Soviet ally in the Cold War.[5]

**Fidel Castro, Havana, Cuba
January 10, 1959**

Photograph by Lester Cole
© Lester Cole/Corbis

Psychiatric Personality Study of Fidel Castro, December 1961, prepared by the Psychiatric Staff of the Central Intelligence Agency, pages 1, 2

" Fidel Castro is not "crazy" but he is so highly neurotic and unstable a personality as to be quite vulnerable to certain kinds of psychological pressure. The outstanding neurotic elements in his personality are his hunger for power and his need for the recognition and adulation of the masses.

Although he depends on the masses for support, he has no real regard for them and does not trust them sufficiently to hold elections. His first consideration is to maintain power control for himself. He probably would destroy both himself and the Cuban people to preserve this status. This is the basis for his continuing the revolutionary stage beyond its period of usefulness. "

John F. Kennedy Presidential Library and Museum, Boston, Massachusetts

December 1961

CENTRAL INTELLIGENCE AGENCY
Psychiatric Staff

SECRET

1 DEC 1961

S-E-C-R-E-T

PSYCHIATRIC PERSONALITY STUDY OF FIDEL CASTRO

I. Psychiatric Summary

Fidel Castro is not "crazy," but he is so highly neurotic and unstable a personality as to be quite vulnerable to certain kinds of psychological pressure. The outstanding neurotic elements in his personality are his hunger for power and his need for the recognition and adulation of the masses. He is unable to obtain complete emotional gratification from any other source.

Castro has a constant need to rebel, to find an adversary, and to extend his personal power by overthrowing existing authority. Whenever his self-concept is slightly disrupted by criticism, he becomes so emotionally unstable as to lose to some degree his contact with reality. If significant vulnerable aspects of his personality were consistently attacked by those he now looks to for approval, the result could be personality disorganization and ineffectuality -- possibly even clinical emotional illness. This illness would probably be depression or some variant of depression, such as an overexcited state, an addiction, or an increase in suspicion to the point of complete withdrawal from reality.

Castro's egoism is his Achilles heel. The extreme narcissistic qualities of his personality are so evident as to suggest predictable patterns of action during both victory and defeat. When he is winning, he must control the situation himself without delegation of authority, and he must continue to seek new areas of authority to overthrow. When faced with defeat, his first concern is to retreat strategically to a place where he can regroup his assets and personally lead another rebellion.

Castro's aggressiveness stems from constant attempts to achieve a special position that is denied him. When he achieves what he desires, he needs constant reassurance that he is justified in occupying this special position. In the past he has sought approval from varying sources but currently he is wringing it from the Cuban masses, the current source of his sense of power and prestige. As long as the masses continue to support him, he will not suffer from anxiety, depression, or overt psychiatric symptoms. The chronic threat to the equilibrium of his personality is that this source of gratification might be withdrawn.

Overtaking the Soviet Union: The Space Race and the Arms Race

During the 1960 Presidential race, Kennedy had campaigned hard on the issue of American strength. The power and prestige of the United States was slipping, he had warned. The Soviet Union had surged ahead of the United States with spectacular achievements in space, and there was a debate within the U.S. intelligence community and concern in Congress as to whether the Soviet Union held the advantage over the United States in strategic weapons. But by 1961, the United States had caught up to the Soviet Union in the space race, and intelligence revealed that it was the United States—not the Soviet Union—that held the advantage in the strategic arms race.

> **Khrushchev:** *This is what America is capable of? And how long has she existed? 300 years? 150 years of independence and this is her level?*
>
> *We haven't quite reached 42 years, and in another 7 years, we'll be at the level of America.*
>
> *And after that, we'll go farther.*
>
> *As we pass you by, we'll wave "hi" to you and then if you want, we'll stop and say, "please come along behind us."*

Soviet Premier Khrushchev (left) and Vice President Richard Nixon at the American National Exhibition in Moscow, July 24, 1959

Photograph by Howard Sochurek

© Time & Life Pictures/ Getty Images

On July 24, 1959, while touring the U.S. American National Exhibition in Moscow, then-Vice President Richard Nixon and Soviet Premier Nikita Khrushchev held an impromptu debate in which the Soviet leader extolled the advantages of communism and boasted of his nation's technological superiority.

President John F. Kennedy delivers a statement on nuclear testing to the nation, November 2, 1961.

John F. Kennedy Presidential Library and Museum, Boston, Massachusetts [KN-C19317]

On November 2, 1961, in a statement made in response to Soviet testing of nuclear weapons, President Kennedy asserted U.S. superiority in nuclear power over the Soviet Union and over "any other nation on earth."

We have many times more nuclear power than any other nation on earth . . . It is essential to the defense of the Free World that we maintain this relative position.

President Kennedy, November 2, 1961

(Drafting Office and Officer)

DEPARTMENT OF STATE

Memorandum of Conversation

DATE: June 4, 1961
3:15 P.M.
Soviet Embassy
Vienna

SUBJECT: Vienna Meeting Between The President
And Chairman Khrushchev.

PARTICIPANTS: The President   Chairman Khrushchev
D - Mr. Akalovsky   Mr. Sukhodrev, Interpreter,
(interpreting)   USSR Ministry of Foreign
Affairs

COPIES TO: The White House
The Secretary
Mr. Kohler
Permanent record copy for the
Executive Secretariat's conference file

After lunch, the President said he wanted to have a few words with the Chairman in private.

The President opened the conversation by saying that he recognized the importance of Berlin and that he hoped that in the interests of the relations between our two countries, which he wanted to improve, Mr. Khrushchev would not present him with a situation so deeply involving our national interest. Of course, he recognized that the decision on Berlin, as far as the USSR was concerned, was with the Chairman. The President continued by saying that evolution is taking place in many areas of the world and no one can predict which course it would take. Therefore, it is most important that decisions be carefully considered. Obviously the Chairman will make his judgment in the light of what he understands to be the best interests of his country. However, the President said, he did want to stress the difference between a peace treaty and the rights of access to Berlin. He reiterated

---

Meeting Face to Face: The Vienna Summit, June 3–4, 1961

The only time President Kennedy and Soviet Premier Khrushchev formally met face-to-face was a summit meeting in Vienna, Austria, June 3–4, 1961. The meetings were tough and contentious, covering a range of issues, both strategic and ideological. Khrushchev's combative posture took President Kennedy by surprise. Neither side yielded a point, and Khrushchev left Kennedy with an ultimatum that signaled a new crisis over the future of Berlin, Hitler's former capital that had been divided between East and West after World War II. Nevertheless, the summit provided an opportunity for both leaders to meet and size up each other as a negotiating adversary.

As a result of Khrushchev's intransigence in Vienna, JFK authorized that the launch sites for the Jupiter intermediate-range ballistic missiles (IRBMs) in Turkey become fully operational—that is, capable of launching missiles that could reach the U.S.S.R. in just minutes.[6]

USSR. It is up to the US to decide whether there will be war or peace. This, he said, can be told Macmillan, De Gaulle and Adenauer. The decision to sign a peace treaty is firm and irrevocable and the Soviet Union will sign it in December if the US refuses an interim agreement.

The President concluded the conversation by observing that it would be a cold winter.

Official Memorandum of Conversation between President Kennedy and Chairman Khrushchev at the Soviet Embassy in Vienna, Austria June 4, 1961

At the Vienna Summit, Khrushchev persisted in the Soviet Union's longtime effort to drive the United States and all the western powers from West Berlin. Khrushchev announced his intention to cut off western access to Berlin and threatened war if the United States or its allies tried to stop him.[7] The President held his ground, affirming U.S. national interests in Berlin, and concluded the meeting saying, "It's going to be a cold winter."

Arriving back at the White House on June 6, 1961, JFK asked the Pentagon for estimates on how many Americans would die in a nuclear war. The response: 70 million Americans—roughly half the nation.[8]

John F. Kennedy Presidential Library and Museum, Boston, Massachusetts

President Kennedy and Chairman Khrushchev at the American Embassy residence in Vienna, Austria, June 3, 1961

[PX-96-33:12]

Chairs used by President Kennedy and Chairman Khrushchev at the American Embassy residence in Vienna, Austria, June 3, 1961

Photograph by Joel Benjamin

President Kennedy purchased these chairs from the State Department for their historic significance and had them shipped to the White House; he intended to donate them to his Presidential Library, where they remain today.

John F. Kennedy Presidential Library and Museum, Boston, Massachusetts

A Threat 90 Miles from Home

*This nation . . . must take an even closer and more realistic look at
the menace of external communist intervention and domination in
Cuba. The American people are not complacent about Iron Curtain
tanks and planes less than 90 miles from our shores.*

President John F. Kennedy, April 20, 1961[9]

As tensions were increasing between the United States and the Soviet
Union, the United States had also been watching the Cuban Revolution with grow-
ing concern. Relations between the two countries deteriorated as the Cuban government expropriated U.S. properties, repressed all dissent, escalated its anti-American
rhetoric, and built an alliance with the Soviet Union. "Cuba appears to be in the process of falling under the domination of International Communism," warned the U.S.
Chief of Naval Operations, and that would present "a direct threat to the security
of the United States."[10] In March 1960, President Dwight D. Eisenhower approved
a $4.4 million program whose purpose was to "bring about the replacement of the
Castro regime with one more devoted to the interest of the Cuban people and more
acceptable to the United States."[11] President Kennedy continued and expanded that
program, which was ultimately codenamed "Operation Mongoose."

The Bay of Pigs Invasion

The Bay of Pigs invasion was the failed attempt by U.S.-backed Cuban exiles to overthrow the government of Fidel Castro. In March 1960, the Eisenhower administration authorized a CIA program to train Cuban exiles as guerrillas. In the final weeks of the Eisenhower administration, the number of exiles under CIA training in Guatemala grew, and the goal became a large-scale invasion. President Kennedy approved of the policy but had doubts about the operation. He wanted it to succeed without a U.S. military invasion and without revealing the U.S. role in organizing the exiles. These objectives proved unrealistic.

The operation was a disaster. Although it was not clear that the plan would ever have worked, President Kennedy's assumption that he would cut the number of planned attacks by U.S.-supplied airplanes to hide the hand of the United States ensured that Castro's air force could harass the invading Cuban exiles.[12]

"Large artillery pieces are shown firing on Cuban rebels as they invade a beachhead in Cuba," April 1961

On April 17, 1961, a 1,400-man invasion force of anti-Castro Cuban exiles, Brigade 2506, landed at the Bay of Pigs beach on the south coast of Cuba. Overwhelmed by a counterattack of Castro's armed forces, the invasion force was crushed two days later. More than 100 men were killed, and nearly 1,100 were taken prisoner and held in Cuba for close to two years.

© Bettman/Corbis/AP Images

. . . there are from this sobering episode useful lessons for all to learn . . . it is clear that the forces of communism are not to be underestimated, in Cuba or anywhere in the world. The advantages of a police state—its use of mass terror and arrests to prevent the spread of free dissent—cannot be overlooked. . . . If the self-discipline of the free mind cannot match the iron discipline of the mailed [sic] fist . . . then the peril to freedom will continue to rise.

6

The Cuban people have not yet spoken their final piece -- and I have no doubt that they *and the Revolutionary Council, led by Dr. Cardona* will continue to speak up for a free and independent Cuba.

Meanwhile, We will not accept Mr. Castro's attempts to blame this nation for the hatred with which his one-time/supporters now regard his repression. But there are from this sobering episode useful lessons for all to learn. Some may still be obscure, and await further information. Some are clear today.

First, it is clear that the forces of communism are not to be underestimated, in Cuba or anywhere in the world. The advantages of a police state -- its use of mass terror and arrests to prevent the

7

spread of free dissent -- cannot be overlooked by those who expect the fall of every fanatic tyrant. If the self-discipline of the free mind cannot match the iron discipline of the mailed fist -- in economic, political, scientific and all other kinds of struggles as well as military -- then the peril to freedom will continue to rise.

Secondly, it is clear that this nation, in concert with all the free nations of this Hemisphere, must take an even closer and more realistic look at the menace of external communist intervention and domination in Cuba. The American people are not complacent about Iron Curtain tanks and planes less than 90 miles from our shores.

President Kennedy's reading copy of his address before the American Society of Newspaper Editors on the failed Bay of Pigs invasion, April 20, 1961, selected pages

Publicly, President Kennedy took responsibility for the invasion's failure and spoke of the lessons to be learned from "this sobering episode." Privately, he wondered aloud to a close adviser, "How could I have been so off base? . . . All my life I've known better than to depend on the experts. How could I have been so stupid, to let them go ahead?"[13]

John F. Kennedy Presidential Library and Museum, Boston, Massachusetts

"Operation Mongoose"

After the failed Bay of Pigs invasion, the CIA's covert action plans for Cuba would be reviewed by a committee of the National Security Council, known as the Special Group Augmented (SGA).[14] Under the guidance of Attorney General Robert F. Kennedy, the President's brother, the SGA directed "Operation Mongoose," which grew to have an annual budget of $50 million and a corps of some 400 agents engaged in a variety of covert operations, including attempts on Castro's life.[15]

~~TOP SECRET~~SENSITIVE

OFFICE OF THE SECRETARY OF DEFENSE
WASHINGTON 25, D. C.

20 February 1962

EYES ONLY

EYES ONLY OF ADDRESSEES

FROM: Brig. Gen. Lansdale _Ed_

SUBJECT: The Cuba Project

      Transmitted herewith is the projection of actions to help Cubans recapture their freedom. This total plan is EYES ONLY. The lives of many brave people depend on the security of this paper entrusted to you. Any inference that this plan exists could place the President of the United States in a most damaging position.

      This is a specific plan, with time phases. It responds to the request of the Special Group (5412) for such a paper. I urge that this paper <u>not</u> be made known, in this complete form, beyond yourself and those named as addressees.

      The Attorney General
      Special Group: General Taylor
      State: Secretary Rusk, Alexis Johnson, Richard Goodwin
      Defense: Secretary McNamara, Deputy Secretary Gilpatric,
            Brig. Gen. Craig   Gen. Lemnitzer
      CIA: John McCone, Richard Helms, William Harvey
      USIA: Ed Murrow, Don Wilson
      White House: President & Bundy

Program review for Operation Mongoose, page 1 (opposite) and transmittal memo from Brig. Gen. Lansdale, February 20, 1962

Brig. Gen. Edward G. Lansdale, Assistant for Special Operations to the Secretary of Defense, acted as chief of operations for the SGA and was the author of the program review. On February 26, 1962, the SGA decided to reduce the scale of the plan set forth here.[16]

"... the United States will help the people of Cuba overthrow the Communist regime from within Cuba and institute a new government with which the United States can live in peace."

John F. Kennedy Presidential Library and Museum, Boston, Massachusetts

SENSITIVE   20 February 1962

Program Review
by Brig. Gen. Lansdale

THE CUBA PROJECT

The Goal. In keeping with the spirit of the Presidential memorandum of 30 November 1961, the United States will help the people of Cuba overthrow the Communist regime from within Cuba and institute a new government with which the United States can live in peace.

The Situation. We still know too little about the real situation inside Cuba, although we are taking energetic steps to learn more. However, some salient facts are known. It is known that the Communist regime is an active Sino-Soviet spearhead in our Hemisphere and that Communist controls inside Cuba are severe. Also, there is evidence that the repressive measures of the Communists, together with disappointments in Castro's economic dependency on the Communist formula, have resulted in an anti-regime atmosphere among the Cuban people which makes a resistance program a distinct and present possibility.

Time is running against us. The Cuban people feel helpless and are losing hope fast. They need symbols of inside resistance and of outside interest soon. They need something they can join with the hope of starting to work surely towards overthrowing the regime. Since late November, we have been working hard to re-orient the operational concepts within the U.S. government and to develop the hard intelligence and operational assets required for success in our task.

The next National Intelligence Estimate on Cuba (NIE 85-62) promises to be a useful document dealing with our practical needs and with due recognition of the sparsity of hard facts. The needs of the Cuba project, as it goes into operation, plus the increasing U.S. capability for intelligence collection, should permit more frequent estimates for our guidance. These will be prepared on a periodic basis.

Premise of Action. Americans once ran a successful revolution. It was run from within, and succeeded because there was timely and strong political, economic, and military help by nations outside who supported our cause. Using this same concept of revolution from within, we must now help the Cuban people to stamp out tyranny and gain their liberty.

On 18 January, the Chief of Operations assigned thirty-two tasks to Departments and Agencies of the U.S. government, in order to provide a realistic assessment and preparation of U.S. capabilities. The Attorney General and the Special Group were apprised of this action. The answers received on 15 February provided the basis for planning a realistic course

THE SOVIET UNION SENDS MISSILES TO CUBA

There will be no big reaction from the U.S. side.

Soviet defense minister on the expected U.S. response to the deployment of nuclear missiles in Cuba.[17]

In January 1961, Khrushchev cited the Cuban Revolution as evidence "of the triumph of socialism and communism on a world scale." [18] But the Caribbean island was both an asset and a vulnerability for the Soviet Union: Cuba's proximity to the United States made it well positioned to be a Soviet military base, but its distance from Moscow meant that Cuba would be hard for the Soviets to defend.

In spring 1962, Khrushchev gambled that the Soviet Union could secretly ship nuclear missiles to Cuba and deceive President Kennedy long enough so that the missiles could become operational. Historians still debate what ultimately prompted Khrushchev to take this huge risk. In his memoirs, Khrushchev gave two reasons, one defensive and one offensive: the defense of the Castro regime in Cuba, and a desire to put pressure on the Kennedy administration by dramatically changing the strategic balance of power. Fragmentary minutes of the Presidium (the Soviet Union's executive governing body), released only in 2002, suggest that initially, at least, the main reason was offensive.[19]

On May 20, a Soviet delegation traveled to Cuba to propose the deployment of nuclear missiles to Cuban officials. On May 30, Castro, who was surprised by the offer, approved it.

Soviet ship *Poltava* enroute to Cuba, September 15, 1962 (detail)

John F. Kennedy Presidential Library and Museum, Boston, Massachusetts [PX66-20-11]

SOVIET SHIP POLTAVA ENROUTE TO CUBA
15 SEPTEMBER 1962

ПОЛТАВА

CHRONOLOGY OF SOVIET DEPLOYMENT OF MISSILES IN CUBA

SPRING 1962 Khrushchev conceives of a plan to secretly deploy nuclear missiles in Cuba. The Presidium approves Khrushchev's proposal.[20] The plan is eventually code-named "Anadyr," the site of a strategic air base in Siberia from which Soviet bombers could reach the United States.[21]

MAY 30, 1962 Cuban leadership accepts the Soviet offer of the missiles; Castro later proposes that the deployment be publicly announced—not carried out in secret—but Khrushchev insists on the operation's secrecy.[22]

SUMMER 1962 U.S. intelligence detects Soviet military shipments to Cuba.[23]

SEPTEMBER 4, 1962 President Kennedy issues a statement warning the Soviet Union that "the gravest issues would arise" if they were to deploy weapons "with significant offensive capability."[24]

SEPTEMBER 7, 1962 President Kennedy calls up 150,000 army reservists for one year of active duty.[25]

THROUGHOUT SEPTEMBER 1962 The Soviet Union repeatedly denies the deployment of offensive weapons.[26] The United States detects more state-of-the-art Soviet defensive surface-to-air-missiles (SAMs) in Cuba and after September 10, decides to limit the amount of time any U-2 will fly over Cuba to lessen the risk of one being shot down.[27]

OCTOBER 4, 1962 The first nuclear warheads arrive in Cuba.[28]

OCTOBER 1962 The Soviet Union continues to deny the presence of offensive weapons in Cuba.

OCTOBER 9, 1962 The United States intensifies surveillance flights over Cuba in an effort to obtain evidence of nuclear missile sites there.[29]

OCTOBER 14, 1962 A U-2 flight flies over the western end of Cuba and photographs activity in San Cristobal.[30]

OCTOBER 15, 1962 Analysts at the National Photographic Interpretation Center (NPIC) find evidence in the photographs of a medium-range ballistic missile site.[31]

OCTOBER 16, 1962 The evidence is presented to President Kennedy.

THE FIRST HARD EVIDENCE OF SOVIET MISSILES IN CUBA

More than 900 images were taken during an aerial photographic reconnaissance mission flown over Cuba on Sunday, October 14, 1962.[32] On October 15, analysts at the National Photographic Interpretation Center concluded that the photographs showed evidence of Soviet missile site construction in Cuba and conveyed their findings to McGeorge Bundy, the President's National Security Adviser.

MRBM FIELD LAUNCH SITE
SAN CRISTOBAL NO 2
14 OCTOBER 1962

TENTS

Early the following morning, Bundy delivered the news and the photographs to the President in his bedroom. Wearing his bathrobe, reviewing newspapers and working papers in preparation for a normal workday, the President learned of the imminent threat to the nation's security. He called a meeting of his foreign policy advisers for 11:45 that morning.[33]

Months later, when JFK asked Bundy why he waited before delivering this news, Bundy explained: "I decided that a quiet evening and a night of sleep were the best preparation you could have."[34]

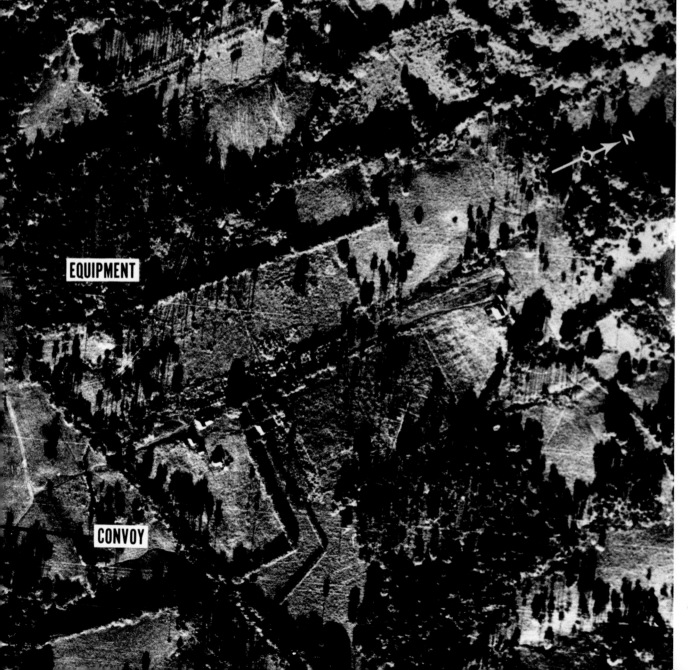

EQUIPMENT

CONVOY

N

19

A Team of Advisers: The "Ex Comm"

Presented with photographic evidence of the missile sites in Cuba, President Kennedy immediately assembled a group of advisers to help formulate a response.

On October 22, he formalized the role of his core advisory group, establishing the Executive Committee of the National Security Council, which became known as the "Ex Comm." Many other advisers and experts participated in the meetings intermittently throughout the crisis.

The President served as chairman of the Committee. Pictured below are the Ex Comm members listed by the President in his Action Memo of October 22 (opposite).

Lyndon B. Johnson
Vice President

Dean Rusk
Secretary of State

Robert McNamara
Secretary of Defense

Douglas Dillon
Secretary of the Treasury

Robert F. Kennedy
Attorney General

John McCone
Director of Central Intelligence

George Ball
Undersecretary of State

Roswell Gilpatric
Deputy Secretary of Defense

Gen. Maxwell Taylor
Chairman of the Joint Chiefs of Staff

Llewellyn Thompson
Ambassador-at-Large

Theodore Sorensen
Special Counsel

McGeorge Bundy
National Security Adviser

THE WHITE HOUSE

WASHINGTON

October 22, 1962

NATIONAL SECURITY ACTION MEMORANDUM 196

TO:
The Vice President
The Secretary of State
The Secretary of Defense
The Secretary of the Treasury
The Attorney General
The Chairman, Joint Chiefs of Staff
The Director of Central Intelligence

SUBJECT   Establishment of an Executive Committee
of the National Security Council

I hereby establish, for the purpose of effective conduct
of the operations of the Executive Branch in the current
crisis, an Executive Committee of the National Security
Council. This committee will meet, until further notice,
daily at 10:00 a.m. in the Cabinet Room. I shall act as
Chairman of this committee, and its additional regular
members will be as follows: the Vice President, the
Secretary of State, the Secretary of Defense, the
Secretary of the Treasury, the Attorney General, the
Director of Central Intelligence, the Under Secretary
of State, the Deputy Secretary of Defense, the Chairman
of the Joint Chiefs of Staff, the Ambassador-at-Large,
the Special Counsel, and the Special Assistant to the
President for National Security Affairs.

The first meeting of this committee will be held at the
regular hour on Tuesday, October 23rd, at which point
further arrangements with respect to its management
and operation will be decided.

cc:
The Under Secretary of State
The Deputy Secretary of Defense
The Ambassador-at-Large
The Special Counsel
The Special Assistant to the President
   for National Security Affairs
bc:
Mr. O'Donnell
Mr. Salinger

CC: Mrs. Lincoln
      Mr. Bundy (3)
      Mr. Johnson
      NSC Files

National Security Action
Memorandum 196, establishing
an Executive Committee of
the National Security Council,
known as the "Ex Comm,"
October 22, 1962

The Ex Comm deliberates in the
White House Cabinet Room,
October 29, 1962

Photograph by Cecil Stoughton

*John F. Kennedy Presidential
Library and Museum,
Boston, Massachusetts
[ST-A26-18-62]*

SECRET RECORDINGS AT THE WHITE HOUSE

For two weeks, the Ex Comm met almost continuously, sorting through the confusion of ever-changing reports and intelligence. With the President guiding the discussions, they argued heatedly—passionately—over the best course of action. As they struggled to make sense of events unfolding around the globe, and the world moved closer to a possible nuclear confrontation, the President made his decisions, imposing them, when necessary, on his advisers.

Unbeknownst to almost all the participants, JFK recorded those White House meetings. Portions selected from the 43 hours of tape transcripts are included in this publication. The tapes are preserved by the John F. Kennedy Presidential Library and Museum in Boston, Massachusetts.

During summer 1962, President Kennedy asked Secret Service Agent Robert Bouck to install a secret tape recording system inside the White House. Two reel-to-reel machines were installed in the basement of the White House West Wing. Concealed microphones were placed inside the President's Oval Office and the Cabinet Room. The President could activate the recording device with controls that were, like the microphones, concealed. In September 1962, a separate taping system, using a device known as a Dictaphone, was installed in the Oval Office to record the President's telephone conversations as well as his dictation.[35]

The secret taping system in the White House recorded nearly 250 hours of White House meetings, including most of the ones that took place almost continuously throughout the Cuban Missile Crisis.[36] The tapes provide entrée to the high-level secret meetings that would determine the U.S. response to the missile crisis. Listeners hear the President's advisory group reacting to events in real time and can discern the moments in which the President makes pivotal decisions.

The President's brother, Attorney General Robert F. Kennedy, knew about the taping system. But when the existence of the tapes became public in 1973, 10 years after the President's death, other trusted advisers and White House insiders were astounded to learn that secret meetings in which they participated had been recorded.

There is no evidence that reveals the President's purpose in creating these tapes.

Tandberg tape recorder, ca. 1960, similar to the one installed by the Secret Service, as directed by the President, to tape conversations in the Cabinet Room and Oval Office

The switch to turn the recorder on was installed on the underside of the conference table in front of the President's chair; the microphones were on the wall directly behind the President's chair in spaces that once held light fixtures.[37]

[ST-A26-1-62]

The President meeting with his advisers in the Cabinet Room, October 29, 1962

John F. Kennedy Presidential Library and Museum, Boston, Massachusetts

TUESDAY, OCTOBER 16

The White House Recordings: The President Assembles His Advisers in the White House Cabinet Room

We do not believe they are ready to fire.

Sidney Graybeal, Missile and Space Division Chief, CIA

The President and his advisers were briefed by CIA officials on the photographic evidence of the Soviet missile deployment in Cuba: images showing the presence of medium-range ballistic missiles (MRBMs). MRBMs had a target range of approximately 1,000 miles, with Washington, DC; Dallas, Texas; and Cape Canaveral, Florida, all falling within that range. Transcripts of Kennedy's tape recordings reveal the Ex Comm's efforts to interpret the evidence.

MARSHALL CARTER: This is the result of the photograph taken Sunday, sir. There's a medium-range ballistic missile launch site and two new military encampments. . . .

The launch site at one of the encampments contains a total of at least 14 canvas-covered missile trailers measuring 67 feet in length, 9 feet in width. The overall length of the trailers plus the tow bars is approximately 80 feet. The other encampment contains vehicles and tents but with no missile trailers.

ARTHUR LUNDAHL: These are the launchers here. Each of these are places we discussed. In this instance the missile trailer is backing up to the launching point. The launch point of this particular vehicle is here. . . .

JFK: How do you know this is a medium-range ballistic missile?

5.4 feet

BOOSTER
59.6 feet

LUNDAHL: The length, sir. . .

JFK: The what? The length?

LUNDAHL: The length of it, yes.

JFK: The length of the missile? Which part? . . .

LUNDAHL: Mr. Graybeal, our missile man, has some pictures of the equivalent Soviet equipment that has been dragged through the streets of Moscow that can give you some feel for it, sir.

SIDNEY GRAYBEAL: There are two missiles involved. One of them is our SS-3, which is 630-mile [range] and on up to near 700. It's 68 feet long. These missiles measure out to be 67 foot long. The other missile, the 1,100 [mile range] one is 73 foot long. . . . It would have to be fired from a stable, hard surface. This could be packed earth. It could be concrete or asphalt. . . .

ROBERT McNAMARA: Would you care to comment on the position of nuclear warheads. This is in relation to the question from the President—when can these be fired?

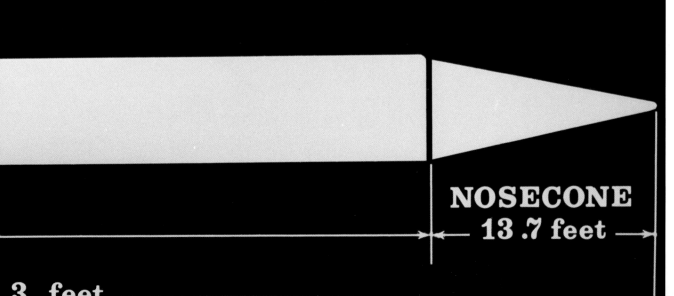

SOVIET MRBM—SANDAL SS-4 (detail)

The presence and size of the missiles was presumptive of nuclear capability.

John F. Kennedy Presidential Library and Museum, Boston, Massachusetts [PX 66-20-10]

GRAYBEAL: Sir, we've looked very hard. We can find nothing that would spell nuclear warhead in terms of any isolated area or unique security in this particular area. The mating of the nuclear warhead to the missile from some of the other short-range missile data—would take about a couple of hours to do this. . . .

The first of the warheads had arrived October 4.[38]

GRAYBEAL: We do not believe they are ready to fire.

NOSECONE 13.7 feet

3.3 feet

Robert Kennedy later recalled seeing the photographs for the first time:

[The experts] told us that if we looked carefully, we could see there was a missile base being constructed. . . . I, for one, had to take their word for it. I examined the pictures carefully, and what I saw appeared to be no more than the clearing of a field. . . . I was relieved to hear later that this was the same reaction of virtually everyone at the meeting, including President Kennedy.[39]

Opposite:

MRBM Field Launch Site, San Cristobal No. 1, 14 October 1962

[PX-66-20-7]

Below:

Map of Cuba used and annotated by President Kennedy when he was first briefed by the CIA on the Cuban Missile Crisis

John F. Kennedy Presidential Library and Museum, Boston, Massachusetts

MRBM FIELD LAUNCH SITE
SAN CRISTOBAL NO 1
14 OCTOBER 1962

ERECTOR/LAUNCHER EQUIPMENT

ERECTOR/LAUNCHER EQUIPMENT

8 MISSILE TRAILERS

EQUIPMENT

TENT AREAS

**President Kennedy confers with
Secretary of Defense McNamara
and Deputy Secretary of Defense
Gilpatric, October 29, 1962**

*John F. Kennedy Presidential
Library and Museum,
Boston, Massachusetts
[ST-A26-23-62]*

The President Considers the Options

In the early days of the crisis, discussions focused generally on three possible courses of action: military strike, diplomatic negotiation, or the institution of a blockade to prevent Soviet ships carrying military equipment from reaching Cuba.

The President's advisory group was split into small sub-groups to discuss the options. They met almost continuously, and their debates were heated. At first, the only point on which all could agree is that some action must be taken: the Soviet missile deployment could not be tolerated.

The President received their written recommendations.[40]

. . . the survival of our nation demands the prompt elimination of the offensive weapons now in Cuba. . . . I recognize fully the public opinion difficulties involved in a surprise attack but believe that, if no other effective course is available, they must be accepted rather than run the grave risk to our national security involved in allowing the weapons to remain in Cuba.

Douglas Dillon, Secretary of the Treasury, to President Kennedy, ca. October 17, 1962[41]

. . . it should be clear as a pikestaff that the U.S. was, is and will be ready to negotiate the elimination of bases and anything else; that it is they who have upset the precarious balance in the world in arrogant disregard of your warning . . . and that we have no choice except to restore that balance, i.e., blackmail and intimidation never, negotiation and sanity always.

Adlai Stevenson, U.S. Ambassador to the United Nations, to President Kennedy, October 17, 1962[42]

I am persuaded that the disadvantages of an air strike are too great for us to undertake. I have, therefore, concluded that the blockade plan—while by no means wholly satisfactory—is the course we should follow.

George W. Ball, Undersecretary of State, ca. October 18, 1962[43]

THURSDAY, OCTOBER 18

The White House Recordings: The President and His Advisers Consider the Options

Is there anyone here who doesn't think that we ought to do something about [the missiles]?

President John F. Kennedy

Most Ex Comm meetings began with an intelligence update delivered by John McCone, Director of Central Intelligence. On October 18, he reported that photo analysts found evidence of site construction for intermediate-range ballistic missiles (IRBMs). With a target range of nearly 2,200 miles, nearly twice as large an area as the range of the MRBMs, IRBMs in Cuba would pose a threat to all parts of the United States, except for the northwest Pacific coast.[44]

In this excerpt, the Ex Comm weighs the impact of a military strike against the missile sites.

McNAMARA: If there is a strike without a preliminary discussion with Khrushchev, how many Soviet citizens will be killed? I don't know. It'd be several hundred at absolute minimum.

McGEORGE BUNDY: Killed as in casualties?

McNAMARA: Killed. Absolutely. We're using napalm, 750-pound bombs. This is an extensive strike we're talking about. . . . I think we must assume we'll kill several hundred Soviet citizens. Having killed several hundred Soviet citizens, what kind of response does Khrushchev have open to him? It seems to me that it just must be a strong response, and I think we should expect that. And, therefore, the question really is are we willing to pay some kind of a rather substantial price to eliminate these missiles? I think the price is going to be high—it may still be worth paying to eliminate the missiles. But I think we must assume it's going to be high. The very least it will be will be to remove the missiles in Italy and Turkey. I doubt we could settle [the problem] for that. . . .

GEORGE BALL: A course of action where we strike without warning is like Pearl Harbor. It's the kind of conduct that one might expect of the Soviet Union. It is not conduct that one expects of the United States. . . .

JFK: Well, let me ask you this. Is there anyone here who doesn't think that we ought to do something about them?

THE WHITE HOUSE

I now know how Tojo felt when he was planning Pearl Harbor.

Remarks by Bobby at meeting Oct. 16, 1962

Note handwritten by Attorney General Robert F. Kennedy during the October 16, 1962, meeting, facsimile

" I now know how Tojo felt when he was planning Pearl Harbor. "

Defense Secretary Robert McNamara later wrote that JFK opposed launching a surprise military strike, in part, because it was "contrary to our traditions and ideals, and an act of brutality for which the world would never forgive us."[45]

Some compared this tactic to Japan's December 7, 1941, surprise attack on the United States at Pearl Harbor, ordered by Japanese Prime Minister Hideki Tojo. George Ball, Undersecretary of State, said, "A course of action where we strike without warning is like Pearl Harbor. It's the kind of conduct that one might expect of the Soviet Union. It is not conduct that one expects of the United States."[46]

Following a late-night meeting with his advisers that took place in the White House residence on October 18, President Kennedy walked over to the Oval Office and recorded a summary of the day's discussions, describing how opinions had shifted during the many hours of discussions and debates. But by the end of the day, the group had moved towards a consensus:

. . . During the course of the day, opinions had obviously switched from the advantages of a first strike on the missile sites and on Cuban aviation to a blockade. . . . The consensus was that we should go ahead with the blockade beginning on Sunday night. Originally we should begin by blockading Soviets against the shipment of additional offensive capacity, [and] that we could tighten the block-ade as the situation requires. I was most anxious that we not have to announce a state of war existing, because it would obviously be bad to have the word go out that we were having a war rather than that it was a limited blockade for a limited purpose.

It was determined that I should go ahead with my speeches so that we don't take the cover off this, and come back Saturday night [October 20].

President Kennedy at his desk in the Oval Office, March 1961

Photograph by Jacques Lowe
© *Estate of Jacques Lowe*

FRIDAY, OCTOBER 19

The White House Recordings: The President Meets with His Military Advisers

"You're talking about the destruction of a country."

President John F. Kennedy

Analysts at the National Photographic Interpretation Center came to the following conclusions after studying the reconnaissance photos:

- 2 MRBM sites were already operational and 8 more would be operational within a week.
- 2 sites intended for IRBMs would be operational within 6 to 8 weeks.[47]

The Joint Chiefs of Staff argued that a blockade alone would be a weak response. Air Force Chief of Staff General Curtis LeMay characterized that strategy as "appeasement"—an emotionally charged term that referred to British and French acquiescence to Nazi territorial demands in Europe in the 1930s. The term had become synonymous with cowardice. The Joint Chiefs urged swift military action.

Throughout the Cuban Missile Crisis, President Kennedy and others were convinced that the Soviet deployment of missiles in Cuba was linked to the presence of the United States in West Berlin. President Kennedy believed that if the United States were to take military action against the missile sites in Cuba, the Soviets would respond with military action in West Berlin, a city he had vowed to protect. "The Cuba-Berlin connection is what makes our problem so difficult," the President said at one point.[48] If the Soviets were to take Berlin by force, he said, he would have no alternative but to fire nuclear weapons in response. The fate of Berlin dominated many of the Ex Comm's discussions.

JFK: What do you think their reprisal [against an air strike] would be?

CURTIS LeMAY: I don't think they're going to make any reprisal if we tell them that the Berlin situation is just like it's always been. . . . So I see no other solution. This blockade and political action, I see leading into war. I don't see any other solution for it. It will lead right into war. This is almost as bad as the appeasement at Munich. . . . I just don't see any other solution except direct military intervention right now. . . .

President Kennedy with the Joint Chiefs of Staff, January 15, 1962

Photograph by Cecil Stoughton

Left to right: David Shoup, Marine Corps Commandant; Earle Wheeler, Army Chief of Staff; Curtis LeMay, Air Force Chief of Staff; President Kennedy; Gen. Maxwell Taylor, Chairman of the Joint Chiefs of Staff; George Anderson, Chief of Naval Operations.

John F. Kennedy Presidential Library and Museum, Boston, Massachusetts [ST-A8-1-63]

JFK: They can't do it [accept our attack] any more than we can let these go on without doing something. They can't let us just take out, after all their statements, take out their missiles, kill a lot of Russians and not do anything. . . .

EARLE WHEELER: . . .From a military point of view, the lowest-risk course of action if we're thinking of protecting the people of the United States against a possible strike on us is to go ahead with a surprise air strike, the blockade, and an invasion because these series of actions progressively will give us increasing assurance that we really have got the offensive capability of the Cuban-Soviets cornered. . . . I feel that the lowest risk course of action is the full gamut of military action by us. That's it, sir. . . .

LeMAY: I think that a blockade and political talk would be considered by a lot of our friends and neutrals as being a pretty weak response to this. And I'm sure that a lot of our own citizens would feel that way, too. In other words, you're in a pretty bad fix at the present time.

JFK: What did you say?

LeMAY: You're in a pretty bad fix.

JFK: You're in there with me. Personally. . . .

LeMAY: If you take out the missiles, I think you've got to take out their air along with it, and their radar, and their communications, the whole works. It just doesn't make any sense to do anything but that. . . .

JFK: The problem is not really some war against Cuba. But the problem is part of this worldwide struggle where we face the Communists, particularly, as I say, over Berlin.

JFK: . . . if it isn't today, it's within a year they're going to have enough . . . when we've talked about the number of ICBMs they have. They may not be quite as accurate. [But] they've got enough, they put them on the cities and you know how soon these casualty figures [mount up]—80 million, whether it's 80 or 100—you're talking about the destruction of a country . . .

JFK: Well, let me ask you this. If we go ahead with this air strike, either on the missiles or on the missiles and the planes . . . when could that be ready.

LeMAY: We can be ready for attack at dawn on the 21st [Sunday], that being the earliest possible date. The optimum date would be Tuesday morning [October 23].

This synopsis, drafted for the President while several courses of action were under discussion, includes an announcement of U.S. military air strikes in Cuba, as well as a call for a summit and a pledge that the United States would withdraw its nuclear missiles based in Turkey.[49]

This morning I reluctantly ordered the armed forces to attack and destroy the nuclear build-up in Cuba. . . . action became necessary both to remove the immediate offensive threat to the Americas and to make crystal clear to the Soviet Union that the United States means what it says and is prepared to defend liberty with all the means at its disposal. . . . There should be no doubt on the part of anyone, that, in carrying out this commitment, the US will be prepared to use all the forces at its disposal including nuclear . . .

I ask the people to remain calm, go about your daily business, secure in the knowledge that our freedom loving country will not allow its security to be undermined . . .

SYNOPSIS OF PRESIDENT'S SPEECH

DECLASSIFIED
E. O. 11652, SEC. 3(E), 5(D), 5(E) AND 11
U.S. Archivist NLK-77-1018
BY *my m* NARS. DATE 5-23-78

1. This morning I reluctantly ordered the armed forces

to attack and destroy the nuclear build-up in Cuba.

2. Background of U.S. position re offensive weapons.

3. Catalogue of offensive weapons in Cuba (possible pictures)

Further pictures to be released as soon as possible.

Faced with this situation, action became necessary both

to remove the immediate offensive threat to the Americas and to

make crystal clear to the Soviet Union that the United States

means what it says and is prepared to defend liberty with all

the means at its disposal.

This applies elsewhere in the world as well as in

Cuba. I refer particularly to Berlin. The United States is

fully prepared to live up to its commitments should there be

36

The President Tries to Maintain Secrecy

In the early days of the crisis, the President maintained his normal schedule to avoid arousing public interest. He would not publicly reveal that there was a crisis until he had decided on a response. To maintain the appearance of normalcy, he left Washington on Friday morning, October 19, for a weekend campaign swing through the Midwest and West.

On Saturday morning, when the President received a telephone call from the Attorney General advising him to return to Washington, JFK devised a story about having a cold. From his room at the Sheraton Hotel in Chicago, he scrawled the beginnings of a public statement while speaking with Pierre Salinger, his press secretary.[50]

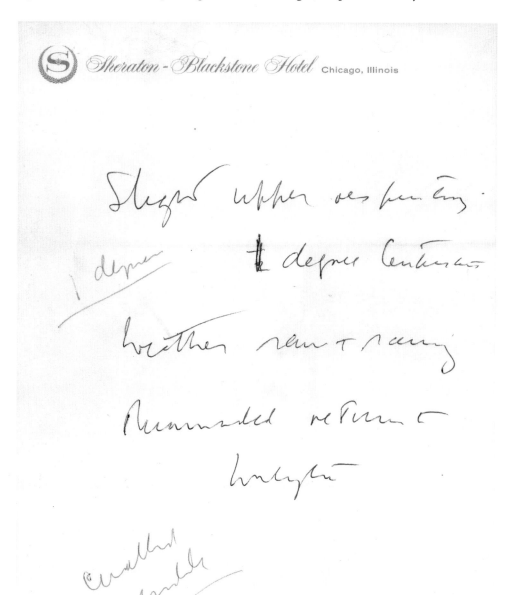

JFK's draft statement explaining his sudden decision to return to Washington, October 20, 1962

" Slight upper respiratory 1 degree temperature Weather raw & rainy Recommended return to Washington Cancelled Schedule "

John F. Kennedy Presidential Library and Museum, Boston, Massachusetts

The White House Recordings: The President Meets with Leaders of Congress

If we go into Cuba . . . we are taking a chance that these missiles, which are ready to fire, won't be fired. . . . is that really a gamble we should take?

President Kennedy

On Saturday afternoon, October 20, the President made his decision. He chose a blockade over military strikes or invasion, with the idea that a blockade was a limited action and that further military steps could be taken later, if necessary. He would address the nation the following Monday evening at 7 p.m., speaking publicly about the national crisis for the first time. Before the announcement, he would meet with congressional leaders to alert them to the situation in Cuba and his response.

Scattered across the country, some key 20 members of Congress were summoned back to Washington for an emergency meeting with the President at the White House. On Monday, October 22, two hours before the President's address to the nation, they entered the Cabinet Room. Alerted to the crisis for the first time, Senator Richard Russell, Majority Leader from Georgia, voiced his concerns about the blockade strategy and urged stronger military action.[51]

Director of Central Intelligence John McCone briefed the congressional leaders:

▮ 4 medium-range ballistic missile sites were in full operational readiness.

▮ 24 medium-range ballistic missile launchers and 12 intermediate-range ballistic launch pads were under construction.

▮ 18 Soviet ships were in Cuban ports; 25 more were on their way.

▮ the Soviets had installed 24 surface-to-air missile bases, several cruise missile defense sites, 40 MiG fighter planes, and 20 IL-28 bombers.

Almost the entire United States was vulnerable to the IRBMs; and the surface-to-air missiles (SAMs) were likely to shoot down an American U-2 reconnaissance plane "within a short time."[52]

RICHARD RUSSELL: Mr. President, I could not stay silent under these circumstances and live with myself. I think that our responsibilities to our people demand stronger steps than that in view of this buildup there, and I must say that in all honesty to myself.

I don't see how we are going to get any stronger or get into any better position to meet this threat. It seems to me that we're at the crossroads. We're either a first-class power or we're not. You have warned these people time and again, in the most eloquent speeches I have read since Woodrow Wilson, as to what would happen if there was an offensive capability created in Cuba. They can't say they're not on notice.

JFK: But, Senator, we can't invade Cuba. . . . We don't have the forces to seize Cuba.

RUSSELL: Well, we can assemble them.

JFK: Well, that's what we're doing now.

RUSSELL: How long?

JFK: OK. Secretary McNamara can describe this. As I say, we just don't have forces there.

Defense Secretary McNamara explains that an invasion would require some 250,000 U.S. military personnel, that airstrikes have to precede an invasion—that it would take at least seven days to carry out those airstrikes: 2,000 bombing sorties against locations occupied by 8,000 Soviet personnel.[53] (The United States had severely underestimated that number: in fact, there were some 42,000 Soviet personnel.)[54]

McNAMARA: I think it's quite remarkable, startlingly so, as a matter of fact, that we can consider an invasion with seven days' preparation. No invasion of this size, that any of my military staff can recall, has ever been prepared with no more than a seven-day lead time. . . .

JFK: If we go into Cuba we have to all realize that we are taking a chance that these missiles, which are ready to fire, won't be fired. So that's a gamble we should take? In any case we are preparing to take it. I think that that is one hell of a gamble. . . . when we finally decide whether we're going to do it, I am going to have everybody in this room be here with us because we ought to decide this one together. . . . In the meanwhile, we are going to move all of the available forces that we have to be in a position to carry out this invasion as quickly as we possibly can. . . . So we may have the war by the next 24 hours.

PRESIDENT KENNEDY ADDRESSES THE NATION, OCTOBER 22, 1962

On October 22, 1962, at 7 p.m., President Kennedy interrupted the nation's Monday night television programs with this public address. In a speech that lasted 17 minutes, he explained that the Soviet Union was in the process of installing nuclear weapons in Cuba. He said that the presence of those missiles so close to the United States would pose a mortal threat to the nation and upset the balance of power between the two superpowers, and that they must be removed. He outlined the steps he was taking in response.

He did not shrink from disclosing the gravity of the threat, but he withheld details of a nuclear strike's full horror.

Customers in a California department store watch President Kennedy's televised address to the nation, as he informs the American people about the unfolding crisis in Cuba, October 22, 1962

Photograph by Ralph Crane

©*Time & Life Pictures/Getty Images*

Good evening, my fellow citizens:

This Government, as promised, has maintained the closest surveillance of the Soviet military build-up on the island of Cuba. Within the past week, unmistakable evidence has established the fact that a series of offensive missile sites is now in preparation on that imprisoned island. The purpose of these bases can be none other than to provide a nuclear strike capability against the Western Hemisphere. Upon receiving the first preliminary hard information of this nature last Tuesday morning at 9 a.m.,

2

I directed that our surveillance be stepped up. And having now confirmed and completed our evaluation of the evidence and our decision on a course of action, this Government feels obliged to report this new crisis to you in full detail.

The characteristics of these new missile sites indicate two distinct types of installations. Several of them INCLUde ~~are~~ Medium Range Ballistic Missiles, capable of carrying a nuclear warhead for a distance of more than 1000 nautical miles. Each of these missiles, in short, is capable of striking Washington, D.C.,

President Kennedy's reading copy of his address to the nation, October 22, pages 1, 2

John F. Kennedy Presidential Library and Museum, Boston, Massachusetts

We will not prematurely or unnecessarily risk the costs of world-wide nuclear war in which even the fruits of victory would be ashes in our mouth—but neither will we shrink from that risk . . . I call upon Chairman Khrushchev to halt and eliminate this clandestine, reckless and provocative threat to world peace . . . He has an opportunity now to move the world back from the abyss of destruction . . .

President Kennedy's address, excerpts

DEFCON-3

While millions of Americans listened spellbound to the President's address, the U.S. military was roused from DEFCON-5, a peacetime military posture, to a heightened alert. At DEFCON-3, the country's fleet of nuclear bombers were dispersed and made ready to be launched within 15 minutes of an order from the President.[55]

On October 24, the Strategic Air Command (SAC), the nation's nuclear arsenal, moved to DEFCON-2—one step from nuclear war. At DEFCON-2, more than 1,400 U.S. bombers loaded with nuclear weapons were on airborne alert, with one-eighth of the bombers in the air at all times—some ready to strike targets inside the Soviet Union. More than 130 Intercontinental Ballistic Missiles (ICBMs), deployed in bunkers and silos across the United States, were also ready for launching.[56]

The nation's massive military machine would remain at this maximum state of military readiness for the next 30 days.

57-M   TOP SECRET

Action   Control: 17398
G   Rec'd: October 23, 1962
                                                           6:55 p.m.
Info   FROM: JCS

SS   TO: Secretary of State
RMR
            NO: 221814Z, October (Army Message)

            PRIORITY

            ACTION CINCAL, CINCLANT, CINCARIB, CINCONAD, USCINCEUR,
            CINCSTRIKE, CINCNELM, CINCSAC, INFORMATION DEPT STATE.

            JCS 6884 from JCS.

            DEFCON 3 is established for US forces world-wide, effective
            222300Z. Reason: Cuban situation. USCINCEUR authorized to
            exercise his discretion in complying with this directive in
            the light of JCS 6830 NOTAL. JCS request that as SACEUR he
            will use his influence with NAC to get NATO to assume
            comparable defense posture. GP-3.

            KEA:2

            NOTE: Advance copies to Mr. Meyers (G) and SS-O 10-23-62 CWO-M

                            TOP SECRET
        • This copy must be returned to RM/R central files with notation of action taken •

ACTION ASSIGNED TO: 6/PM	ACTION TAKEN None Again	
NAME OF OFFICER & OFFICE SYMBOL WBRut	DATE OF ACTION 240ct	DIRECTIONS TO RM/R 2th

Quarantine Proclamation

At 7 p.m., on October 23, President Kennedy signed a Quarantine Proclamation authorizing the naval quarantine of Cuba. It would go into effect at 10 a.m. the next morning. The quarantine line would be a 500-mile radius from the eastern tip of Cuba.[57]

A legal expert at the State Department had suggested that the term "quarantine" would be less belligerent in its connotations, since a blockade was regarded under international law as an act of war.[58]

Quarantine Proclamation: Interdiction of the Delivery of Offensive Weapons to Cuba, signed October 23, 1962, first and last pages

General Records of the U.S. Government National Archives, Washington, DC

INTERDICTION OF THE DELIVERY OF OFFENSIVE
WEAPONS TO CUBA

- - - - - - - - - -

BY THE PRESIDENT OF THE UNITED STATES OF AMERICA
A PROCLAMATION

WHEREAS the peace of the world and the security of the United States and of all American States are endangered by reason of the establishment by the Sino-Soviet powers of an offensive military capability in Cuba, including bases for ballistic missiles with a potential range covering most of North and South America;

WHEREAS by a Joint Resolution passed by the Congress of the United States and approved on October 3, 1962, it was declared that the United States is determined to prevent by whatever means may be necessary, including the use of arms, the Marxist-Leninist regime in Cuba from extending, by force or the threat of force, its aggressive or subversive activities to any part of this hemisphere, and to prevent in Cuba the creation or use of an externally supported military capability endangering the security of the United States; and

WHEREAS the Organ of Consultation of the American Republics meeting in Washington on October 23, 1962, recommended that the Member States, in accordance with Articles 6 and 8 of the Inter-American Treaty of Reciprocal Assistance, take all measures,

- 4 -

In carrying out this order, force shall not be used except in case of failure or refusal to comply with directions, or with regulations or directives of the Secretary of Defense issued hereunder, after reasonable efforts have been made to communicate them to the vessel or craft, or in case of self-defense. In any case, force shall be used only to the extent necessary.

IN WITNESS WHEREOF, I have hereunto set my hand and caused the seal of the United States of America to be affixed.

Done in the City of Washington this twenty-third day of October in the year of our Lord, nineteen hundred and sixty-two, and of the Independence of the United States of America the one hundred and eighty-seventh.

By the President:

Secretary of State

I hope that you will issue immediately the necessary instructions to your ships to observe the quarantine.

President Kennedy to Premier Khrushchev, October 23, 1962

No, Mr. President, I cannot agree to this, and I think that in your own heart you recognize that I am correct. I am convinced that in my place you would act the same way.

Premier Khrushchev to President Kennedy, October 24, 1962

Pen used to sign the Proclamation

Photograph by Joel Benjamin

Often, the President would sign a milestone document with many pens, and then give them away as mementos. But he used only this one pen to sign the quarantine order, and he slipped it into his pocket immediately after, saying "I am going to keep this one."[59]

President Kennedy signing the Quarantine Proclamation, October 23, 1962

Photograph by Abbie Rowe

John F. Kennedy Presidential Library and Museum, Boston, Massachusetts [AR 7558-A]

PREPARING FOR NUCLEAR WAR

I got the conclusion that not very much could or would be done; that whatever was done would involve a great deal of publicity and public alarm.

John McCone, Director of Central Intelligence, after a briefing on the nation's ability to prepare for and withstand a Soviet nuclear attack, October 23, 1962 [60]

In the summer and fall of 1961, as tensions between the United States and the Soviet Union escalated, President Kennedy announced a massive program to build and stock fallout shelters across the country:

In the event of an attack, the lives of those families which are not hit in a nuclear blast and fire can still be saved—if they can be warned to take shelter and if that shelter is available. We owe that kind of insurance to our families—and to our country.[61]

But after consulting more closely with his science advisers, JFK privately became less confident in the ability to dramatically limit casualties with an extensive system of fallout shelters.[62]

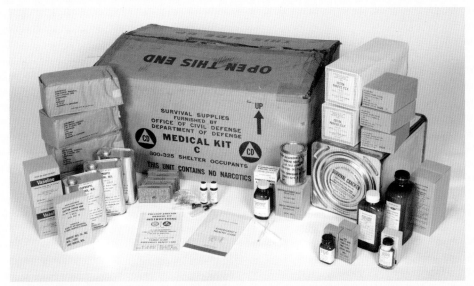

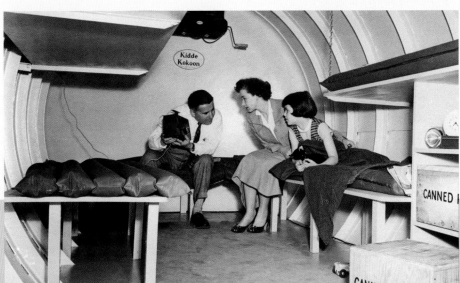

At the height of the Cuban Missile Crisis, the United States was conducting a series of nuclear tests over the Pacific Ocean.[63] The United States began these tests, codenamed "Operation Dominic," in response to a Soviet program of nuclear tests resumed in September 1961 after a three-year moratorium.

Explosion from the nuclear test conducted by the United States, October 18, 1962

Frame capture from the motion picture film "Operation Dominic Nuclear Test, 1962"

Courtesy Department of Energy, Washington, DC

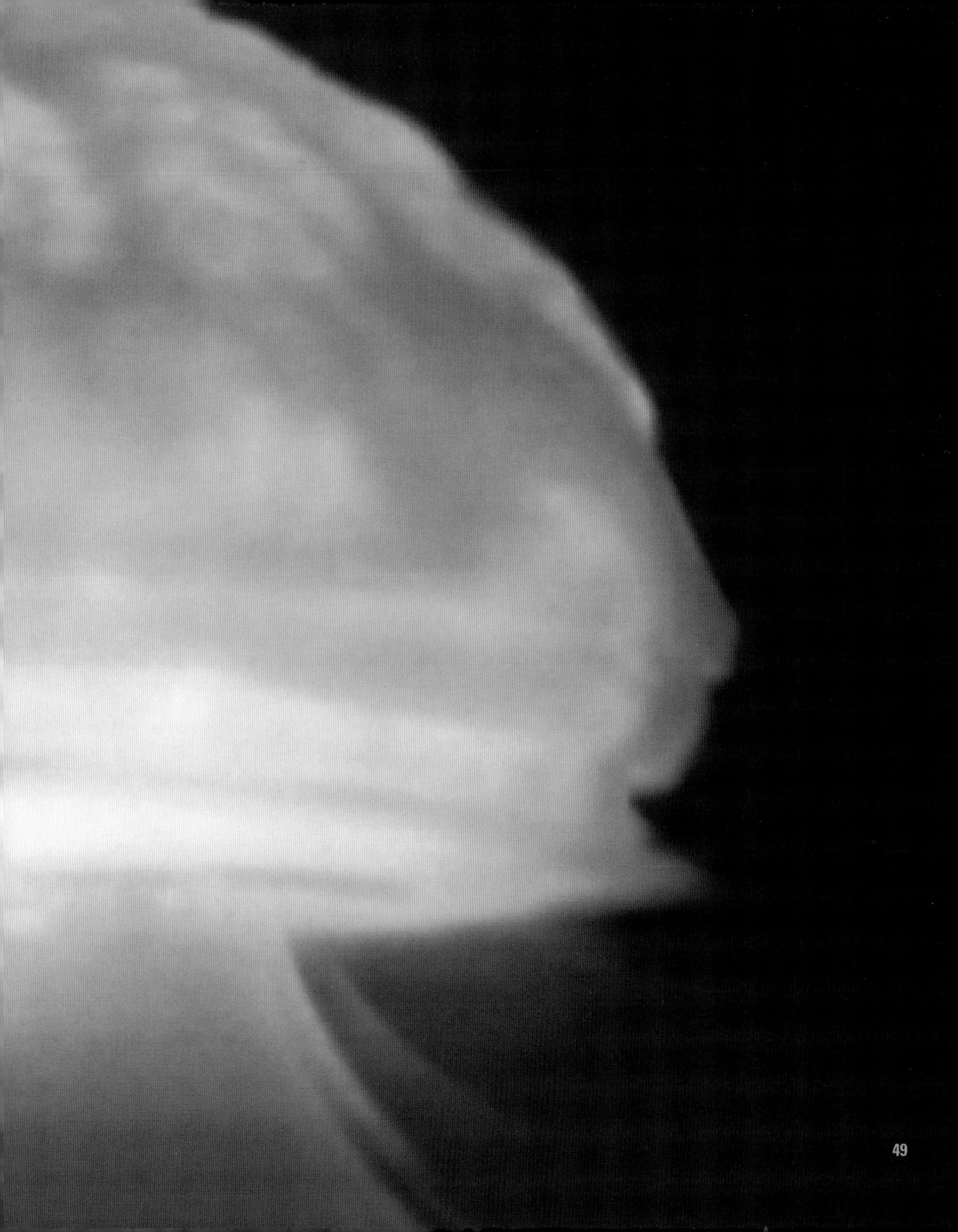

The White House Recordings: Managing a Confrontation at Sea

OK. Let's proceed.

President Kennedy approving the use of small explosives to send a warning signal to Soviet submarines lurking underwater near the quarantine line.[64]

At 10 a.m. Wednesday morning, as the quarantine went into effect, the Ex Comm assembled in the Cabinet Room to discuss how, exactly, it would be implemented. Secretary of Defense McNamara reported that two Soviet ships were approaching the quarantine line; one of them, the *Kimovsk*, had hatches large enough to hold missiles and would be targeted for interception by the USS *Essex* near the quarantine line before noon. Even more ominously, he reported the presence of Soviet submarines that had the ability to sink a U.S. warship. The submarines should be dealt with, he argued, before the Navy attempted to intercept the Soviet ship. McNamara proposed a series of antisubmarine tactics to force the submarines to surface, and as much as the President wanted to avoid hostilities against a Soviet submarine, he approved the use of small explosive "depth charges."[65] Robert Kennedy later described this conversation as one of the tensest moments of the crisis.

In the middle of this discussion, the Ex Comm received word that six of the Soviet ships identified as being "in Cuban waters" had either stopped or reversed course, and the President ordered the USS *Essex* to put a hold on her plans to intercept the Soviet ship. The plan to harass the Soviet submarines with "warning depth charges," however, did proceed.

At this meeting, Director of Central Intelligence John McCone reported that construction on the missile sites was not only progressing, but accelerating; construction on buildings to store nuclear material was proceeding rapidly.[66]

McNAMARA: There are two [Soviet] vessels that I'll be discussing. One is the *Gagarin,* and the other is the *Kimovsk*. . . Both of these will be approaching the barrier, by which I mean, they are about 500 miles from Cuba at approximately noon today. . . . Both of these ships are good targets for our first intercept. Admiral Anderson's plan is to try to intercept one or both of them today. There is a submarine very close, we believe, to each of them. Between. One submarine relatively close to both of them . . .

McCONE: Mr. President, I have a note just handed to me from . . . It says that we've just received information through ONI [US Navy's Office of Naval Intelligence] that all six Soviet ships currently identified in Cuban water. . .have either stopped, or reversed course. . . .

JFK: Why don't we find out whether they're talking about the ships leaving Cuba or the ones coming in? . . .

McNAMARA: Here is the exact situation. We have depth charges that have such a small charge that they can be dropped and they can actually hit the submarine, without damaging the submarine . . . We propose to use those as warning depth charges . . . . The range of our sonar in relation to the range of his torpedo, and the inaccuracy, as you well know, of antisubmarine warfare is such that I don't have any great confidence that we can push him away from our ships and make the intercept securely. . . . this is only a plan and there are many, many uncertainties.

RUSK: Yeah.

JFK: OK, Let's proceed.

Soon after, someone whispers information to the President.

MAXWELL TAYLOR: Three ships are definitely turning back. One is the *Poltava,* we are most interested in. They did not give an additional number that may leave, but they say certain others are showing indications that they may be turning back. Admiral Anderson is making every effort now to get planes out into the area, to have patrols there that will be vectored into this area.

JFK: It seems to me we want to give that specific ship a chance to turn around. You don't want to have word going out from Moscow: "Turn around" and suddenly we sink a ship. So I would think that we ought to be in touch with the [aircraft carrier] *Essex,* and just tell them to wait an hour and see whether that ship continues on its course in view of this other intelligence.

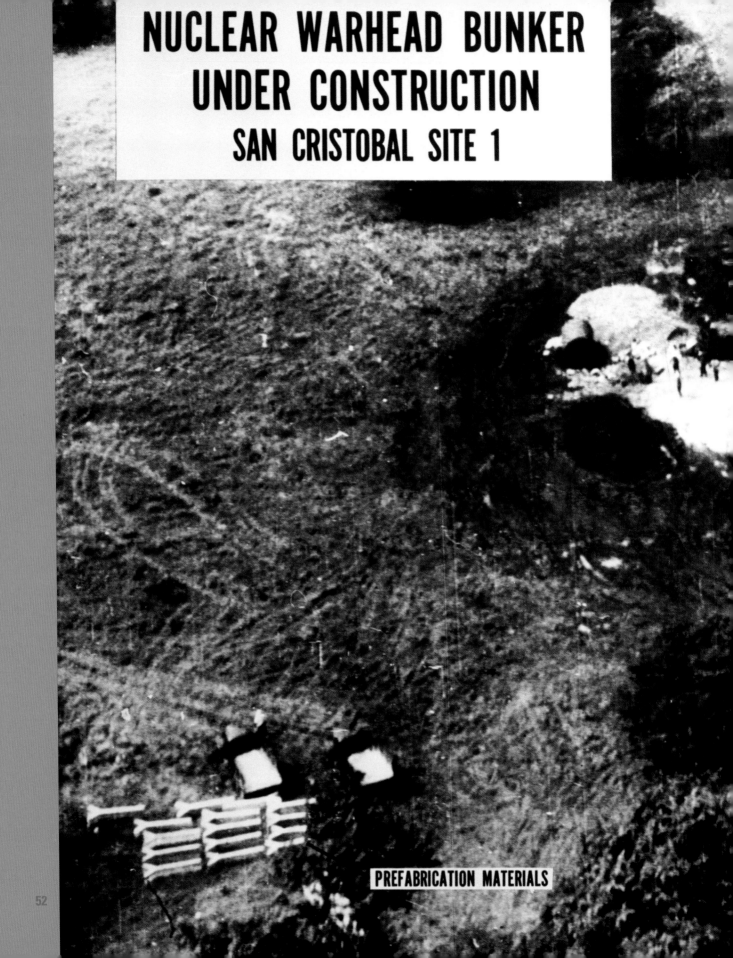

NUCLEAR WARHEAD BUNKER
UNDER CONSTRUCTION
SAN CRISTOBAL SITE 1

PREFABRICATION MATERIALS

**Nuclear Warhead Bunker Under
Construction, San Cristobal
Site 1**

*John F. Kennedy Presidential
Library and Museum,
Boston, Massachusetts
[PX66-20-20]*

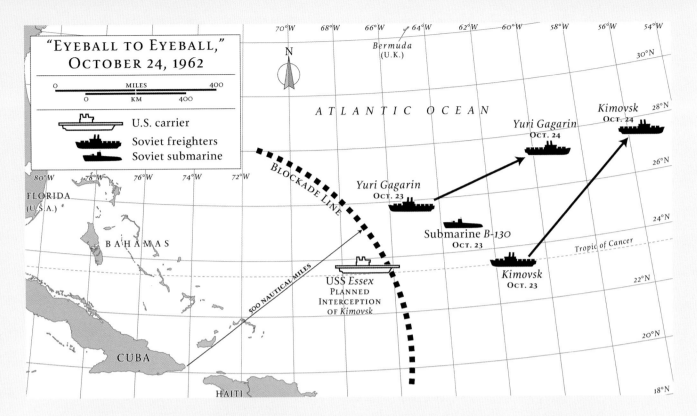

"Eyeball to Eyeball,"
October 24, 1962

Illustration by David Lindroth, published in One Minute to Midnight *by Michael Dobbs*

This map illustrates the reversal of the two Soviet ships, the *Kimovsk* and the *Yuri Gagarin,* that had been targeted for interception by the aircraft carrier USS *Essex* on the first day of the quarantine.

When the Ex Comm learned that the Soviet ships had reversed course, Secretary of State Dean Rusk turned to National Security Adviser McGeorge Bundy and said, "We're eyeball to eyeball, and the other fellow just blinked."[67] In fact, the *Kimovsk* had turned around the previous day, but the Ex Comm did not receive that information until Wednesday morning.[68]

During a discussion on October 25 about 14 Soviet ships that had turned around, President Kennedy cautioned against being overly optimistic: "I don't want a sense of euphoria passing around."[69]

President Kennedy's notes with the word "euphoria," not dated

John F. Kennedy Presidential Library and Museum, Boston, Massachusetts

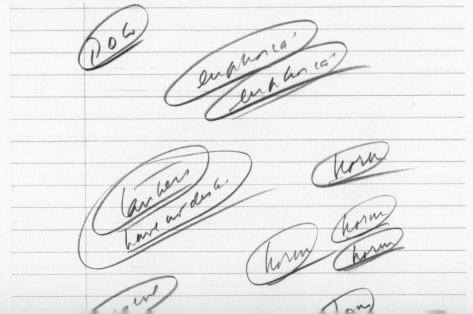

Above:

P2V Neptune U.S. patrol plane flying over a Soviet freighter, October 1962

[428-N-1065352]

Right:

CIA report on Soviet ships en route to Cuba, October 24, 1962

The cover sheet reads:

" *Our present count shows 22 ships en route to Cuba, of which 16 are dry cargo ships and six are tankers. . . . The three ships on the attached list which are asterisked have holds with hatches big enough to accommodate MRBMs or IRBMs.* "

Records of the Central Intelligence Agency
National Archives, Washington, DC

SOVIET SHIPS CURRENTLY EN ROUTE TO CUBA
As of 2100 23 October 1962

	Ship	Latest Position	Type	ETA Havana Area
1.	Aleksandrovsk	22 Oct 1634Z 30:30N, 71:30W	Dry Cargo	25 Oct
2.	Kimovsk*	23 Oct 0700Z 23:20N, 61:30W	Dry Cargo	25 Oct
3.	Vinnitsa	24 Oct 0000Z 24:00N, 70:30W	Tanker	26 Oct
4.	Bucharest	23 Oct 1500Z 26:18N, 53:51W	Tanker	27 Oct
5.	Dolmatovo	23 Oct 1146Z 27:00N, 35:42W	Dry Cargo	28-29 Oct
6.	Grozny	23 Oct 0001Z 27:36N, 37:18W	Tanker	29 Oct
7.	Poltava*	23 Oct 1500Z 35:10N, 59:55W	Dry Cargo	29 Oct
8.	Kislovodsk	23 Oct 1500Z 36:43N, 24:32W	Dry Cargo	31 Oct
9.	Fizik Vavilov	23 Oct 0947Z 35:30N, 07:00W	Dry Cargo	31 Oct-1 Nov
10.	Bolshevik Sukhanov	23 Oct 1500Z	Dry Cargo	1 Nov

WHAT THEY DIDN'T KNOW

We're going to blast them now! We will die, but we will sink them all—we will not disgrace our Navy!

Soviet submarine Captain Valentin Savitsky giving the order to arm a nuclear-tipped torpedo, October 27, 1962

Unbeknownst to the Ex Comm and the U.S. Navy, each of the Soviet submarines was armed with a nuclear-tipped torpedo. Soviet Captain V. P. Orlov of the Soviet submarine B-59 was in charge of the vessel's radio intelligence on October 27 when the U.S. Navy dropped depth charges in an effort to force the submarine to the surface. He later recalled that the temperature inside soared to over 100 degrees, and he described the episode:

It felt like sitting in a metal barrel with someone hitting it with a sledgehammer. . . . It was unbearably stuffy. . . . the duty officers . . . were falling like dominoes. . . . We thought—that's it—the end. . . . Savitsky [the submarine's commander] became furious. He summoned the officer who was assigned to the nuclear torpedo, and ordered him to assemble it to battle readiness. . . . But we did not fire the nuclear torpedo—Savitsky was able to rein in his wrath.[70]

After hours of being subjected to the "depth charges," the Soviet submarine surfaced. Although the Soviet submarine commander was not authorized to launch a nuclear-tipped torpedo without a direct order from Moscow, the incident might possibly have triggered a nuclear confrontation at sea.[71]

A NAVY HELICOPTER HOVERS OVER RUSSIAN SUBMARINE.

The U.S. Navy shadows the second submarine commanded by Savitsky to surface, after repeated rounds of signaling depth charges on October 27, 1962[72]

National Archives, Washington, DC [428-N-711199]

SECRET CORRESPONDENCE: JFK AND KHRUSHCHEV

The two leaders exchanged a series of secret messages as the crisis unfolded, using secure diplomatic channels to communicate directly. Messages were hand-carried, ciphered, deciphered, and translated in a process that created lag times of up to 12 hours. With the world on the brink of a nuclear cataclysm, the two leaders could not communicate in real time.

Н. ХРУЩЕВ

Khrushchev's "Knot of War" Message

Although major hostilities at the quarantine line off the coast of Cuba had thus far been avoided, work on the missile sites continued. On Friday, October 26, Khrushchev received intelligence information indicating that the United States would begin an attack on Cuba within the next two days. He dictated a long and rambling message to President Kennedy signaling that there could be a diplomatic way out of the crisis: he seemed to suggest that if the United States were to agree not to invade Cuba, the missiles could be removed.[73]

This message was delivered to the U.S. Embassy in Moscow at 4:42 p.m. In Washington, it was 9:42 a.m. Diplomats at the U.S. Embassy divided the letter into four parts to facilitate its transmission. The first part arrived at 5 p.m., Washington time; the last close to 9 p.m.—nearly 12 hours after the U.S. Embassy had received it in Moscow.[74]

5c

would also change the approach to the question of destroying not only the armaments which you call offensive, but of every other kind of armament.

I have spoken on behalf of the Soviet Government at the United Nations and introduced a proposal to disband all armies and to destroy all weapons. How then can I stake my claims on these weapons now?

Armaments bring only disasters. Accumulating them damages the economy, and putting them to use would destroy people on both sides. Therefore, only a madman can believe that armaments are the principal means in the life of society. No, they are a forced waste of human energy, spent, more-over, on the destruction of man himself. If people do not display wisdom, they will eventually reach the point where they will clash, like blind moles, and then mutual annihilation will commence.

Let us therefore display statesmanlike wisdom. I propose: we, for our part, will declare that our ships bound for Cuba are not carrying any armaments. You will declare that the United States will not invade Cuba with its tropps and will not support any other forces which might intend to invade Cuba. Then the necessity for the presence of our military specialists in Cuba will be obviated.

Mr. President, I appeal to you to weigh carefully what the aggressive, piratical actions which you have announced the United States intends to carry out in international waters would lead to. You yourself know that a sensible person simply cannot agree to this, cannot recognize your right to such action.

If you have done this as the first step towards unleashing war--well then--evidently nothing remains for us to do but to accept this challenge of yours. If you have not lost command of yourself and realize clearly what this could lead to, then, Mr. President, you and I should not now pull on the ends of the rope in which you have tied a knot of war, because the harder you and I pull, the tighter this knot will become. And a time may come when this knot is tied so tight that the person who tied it is no longer capable of untying it, and then the knot will have to be cut. What that would mean I

need

8

5c

need not explain to you, because you yourself understand perfectly what dread forces our two countries possess.

Therefore, if there is no intention of tightening this knot, thereby dooming the world to the catastrophe of thermonuclear war, let us not only relax the forces straining on the ends of the rope, let us take measures for untying this knot. We are agreeable to this.

We welcome all forces which take the position of peace. Therefore, I both expressed gratitude to Mr. Bertrand Russell, who shows alarm and concern for the fate of the world, and readily responded to the appeal of the Acting Secretary General of the U.N., U Thant.

These, Mr. President, are my thoughts, which, if you should agree with them, could put an end to the tense situation which is disturbing all peoples.

These thoughts are governed by a sincere desire to alleviate the situation and remove the threat of war.

                                        Respectfully,

                                        [s] N. Khrushchev

                                        N. Khrushchev

October 26, 1962

If the President and Government of the United States would give their assurances that the United States would not take part in an attack upon Cuba . . . if you recall your Navy—this would immediately change everything.

If you have not lost command of yourself and realize clearly what this could lead to, then, Mr. President, you and I should not now pull on the end of the rope in which you have tied a knot of war, because the harder you and I pull, the tighter this knot will become. And a time may come when this knot is tied so tight that the person who tied it is no longer capable of untying it, and then the knot will have to be cut. . . . Therefore, if there is no intention of tightening this knot, thereby dooming the world to the catastrophe of thermonuclear war, let us not only relax the forces straining on the ends of the rope, let us take measures for untying this knot.

Уважаемый г-н Президент,

Получил Ваше письмо от 25 октября. Из Вашего письма я почувствовал, что у Вас есть некоторое понимание сложившейся ситуации и сознание ответственности. Это я ценю.

Сейчас мы уже публично обменялись своими оценками событий вокруг Кубы и каждый из нас изложил свое об'яснение и свое понимание этих событий. Поэтому я считал бы, что, видимо, продолжение обмена мнениями на таком расстоянии, пусть даже в виде закрытых писем, вряд ли что-либо добавит к тому, что одна сторона уже сказала другой.

Думаю, Вы правильно поймете меня, если Вы действительно заботитесь о благе мира. Мир нужен всем: и капиталистам, если они не потеряли рассудка, и тем более коммунистам, людям, которые умеют ценить не только свою собственную жизнь, но больше всего - жизнь народов. Мы, коммунисты, вообще против всяких войн между государствами и отстаиваем дело мира с тех пор, как появились на свет. Мы всегда рассматривали войну как бедствие, а не как игру и не как средство для достижения определенных целей и тем более - не как самоцель. Наши цели ясны, а средство их достижения - труд. Война является нашим врагом и бедствием для всех народов.

Так понимаем вопросы войны и мира мы, советские люди, а вместе с нами и другие народы. Это я во всяком случае твердо могу сказать за народы социалистических стран и также за всех прогрессивных людей, которые хотят мира, счастья и дружбы между народами.

Его Превосходительству
Джону КЕННЕДИ,
Президенту Соединенных Штатов
Америки

Эти соображения продиктованы искренним стремлением разрядить обстановку, устранить угрозу войны.

С уважением

Н.ХРУЩЕВ

26 октября 1962 года

A CONFRONTATION AT THE UNITED NATIONS

Even as the United States made military preparations for war, the President and the Ex Comm continued to pursue diplomatic solutions to the crisis. Seeking a show of solidarity with the countries in South and Central America, the United States presented its case to the Organization of American States (OAS), which voted unanimously on October 23 to condemn the Soviet Union and support the United States quarantine.[75]

Back channels—unofficial lines of communication between the United States and the Soviet Union—remained open and active, with intermediaries conveying messages between the two sides outside the more cumbersome and time-consuming State Department channels.

And on October 25, at an emergency meeting of the United Nations Security Council, U.S. Ambassador Adlai Stevenson confronted Soviet Ambassador Valerian Zorin with photographic evidence of the missile site construction in Cuba. It was a dramatic encounter that took place on the world stage, and was broadcast on television and witnessed by millions.[76] These diplomatic initiatives helped to establish a legal justification for the quarantine and to bolster worldwide support for the U.S. position.[77]

U.S. Ambassador Adlai Stevenson (right, seated) and Soviet Ambassador Valerian Zorin (left, seated) inside the United Nations Security Council, October 25, 1962

© Bettman/Corbis/AP Images

From the exchange between U.S. Ambassador Adlai Stevenson and Soviet Ambassador Valerian Zorin at the United Nations, October 25, 1962:

STEVENSON: Do you, Ambassador Zorin, deny that the U.S.S.R. has placed, and is placing medium and intermediate range missiles and sites in Cuba? Yes or no—don't wait for the translation—yes or no.

ZORIN: I am not in an American courtroom, sir, and I do not wish to answer a question put to me in the manner in which a prosecutor does.

STEVENSON: You are in the courtroom of world opinion right now, and you can answer yes or no. You have denied they exist, and I want to know if I understood you correctly.

ZORIN: You will receive your answer in due course. Do not worry.

STEVENSON: I am prepared to wait for my answer until hell freezes over, if that is your decision. . . .

. . . We know the facts, and so do you, sir, and we are ready to talk about them. Our job here is not to score debating points. Our job, Mr. Zorin, is to save the peace. And if you are ready to try, we are.[78]

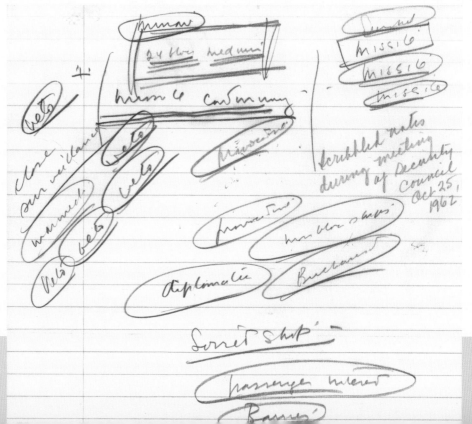

President Kennedy's notes as he watched the U.N. Security Council meeting, October 25, 1962[79]

President Kennedy's secretary, Evelyn Lincoln, annotated these notes.

John F. Kennedy Presidential Library and Museum, Boston, Massachusetts

BLACK SATURDAY, OCTOBER 27, 1962

On October 27, the crisis started to spiral out of control. Events of the previous nine days had unleashed forces that were moving beyond the reach of the only two men who could control them. The day is remembered as "Black Saturday" because of two separate incidents.

Taking off from a U.S. Air Force base in Alaska, an American pilot accidentally strayed into Soviet airspace after losing his bearings while on an air sampling mission over the North Pole. The incident could easily have been interpreted by the Soviets as a provocation—a preliminary reconnaissance mission preceding a nuclear attack on Soviet soil.

Almost simultaneously, an American U-2 plane was shot down over the village of Veguitas by order of two Soviet officers on the ground in Cuba.[80] The pilot died instantly. The Ex Comm assumed—mistakenly—that the order had come from Moscow and interpreted it as a deliberate escalation. The President was urged to order a retaliatory strike against the surface-to-air-missile (SAM) site that had launched the missile; but in a show of restraint, he decided to wait, averting an incident that might have escalated into a nuclear exchange.[81]

Notes of Thomas A. Parrott, CIA Officer assigned to the White House, on the U-2 plane that strayed into Soviet airspace, not dated

Secretary of Defense Robert McNamara learned of the incident at 1:40 p.m., more than an hour-and-a-half after Maultsby crossed the Soviet border; McNamara immediately informed the President by telephone.[82]

" *Was routine air sampling mission from Eilsen (spelling?) AFB, Alaska, north to Pole and back. These stay 100–200 miles from Soviet territory. . . . Apparently gyro trouble developed, and he got off course. . . . Seems to have overflown, or come close to, Soviet territory. Not clear at this time exactly what course was. Russian fighters scrambled—ours too. Now gliding into Kotzebue, Alaska. McNamara talked to Pres.* "

John F. Kennedy Presidential Library and Museum, Boston, Massachusetts

THE WHITE HOUSE
WASHINGTON

Re U-2

Was routine air sampling mission from Eilsen (spelling?) AFB, Alaska, north to Pole and back. These stay 100-200 miles from soviet territory. are not in peripheral recon. program.

apparently gyro trouble developed, and he got off course. Picked up by HFDF (high frequency direction finder) aff

U.S. Plane Strays into Soviet Airspace

Capt. Charles Maultsby, a 36-year-old veteran of the Korean War, planned to fly from Eielson Air Force Base in Alaska to the North Pole and back but accidentally strayed off course, which took him over Soviet territory.

Soviet fighter aircraft from two Siberian airfields, Pevek and Anadyr, scrambled to intercept Maultsby's plane; two U.S. fighter jets, armed with nuclear-tipped missiles, also scrambled to guide Maultsby back to Alaska, where he landed safely at Kotzebue, the site of a U.S. military radar station.[83]

> *Is it not a fact that an intruding American plane could be easily taken for a nuclear bomber.*

Premier Khrushchev to President Kennedy, October 28, 1962

> *The pilot made a serious navigational error which carried him over Soviet territory. . . . I regret this incident and will see to it that every precaution is taken to prevent recurrence.*

President Kennedy to Premier Khrushchev, October 28, 1962

Capt. Charles Maultsby, ca. 1960

Courtesy United States Air Force Thunderbirds Museum, Nellis AFB, Nevada

Charles Maultsby's mission to North Pole, October 27, 1962

This map shows Maultsby's planned route and his actual flight path.

Illustration by David Lindroth, published in One Minute to Midnight *by Michael Dobbs*

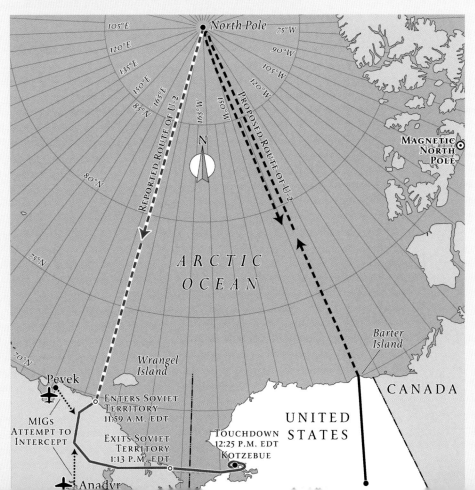

U.S. Plane Shot Down over Cuba

Maj. Rudolf Anderson, Jr., a U.S. Air Force pilot, was the only combat casualty of the Cuban Missile Crisis. He was shot down by a Soviet surface-to-air missile during a reconnaissance flight over Cuba on October 27, 1962, at approximately 10:22 a.m. local time.

Major Anderson had piloted a U-2 mission on October 15 that produced some of the early photographic evidence of the Soviet deployment of missiles.[84] He was posthumously awarded the first Air Force Cross, which cited his "extraordinary heroism . . . during this period of great national crisis."[85]

Maj. Rudolf Anderson, Jr.

National Archives, Washington, DC [342-B-12-004-off]

Draft of President Kennedy's letter to Jane Anderson, widow of Maj. Rudolf Anderson, October 28, 1962

After reading this draft, President Kennedy wrote the following lines:

Your husband's mission was of the greatest importance but I know how deeply you must feel his loss.

Mrs. Anderson gave birth to the couple's third child 7½ months later.[86]

John F. Kennedy Presidential Library and Museum, Boston, Massachusetts

THE WHITE HOUSE

WASHINGTON

28 October 1962

Dear Mrs. Anderson:

I was deeply shocked by the loss of your husband on an operational flight on Saturday, October 27th, 1962.

The courage and outstanding abilities of your husband were evident throughout his career, as witnessed by the award to him during the Korean War, of the Distinguished Flying Cross with two clusters. His tragic loss on a mission of most vital national urgency was once again the sacrifice of a brave and patriotic man. In time of crisis the source of our freedom since the founding days of our country.

On behalf of a grateful nation, I wish to convey to you and your children the sincere gratitude of all the people. I have directed the award of the Distinguished Service Medal to your husband.

Mrs. Kennedy joins me in extending to you our deepest sympathy in the loss of your husband.

Sincerely,

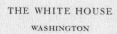

ANTIAIRCRAFT SITE
EAST OF SAN CRISTOBAL MRBM SITE 1
27 OCTOBER 1962

RANGE FINDER

57-MM ANTIAIRCRAFT GUN

RADAR

VAN

**Antiaircraft Site, East of
San Cristobal MRBM Site 1,
October 27, 1962**

*John F. Kennedy Presidential
Library and Museum,
Boston, Massachusetts
[PX66-20-17]*

65

OCTOBER 27, 1962

The White House Recordings: Black Saturday

Time ticks away on us.

President Kennedy

The Ex Comm met almost continuously throughout Saturday, October 27. The President and his advisers tried to untangle their confusion over two conflicting messages from Khrushchev. They tried to interpret the meaning of Major Anderson's U-2 plane being shot down over Cuba: was it a deliberate escalation by the Soviets, or not? And the Ex Comm discussed how to allay the Soviets' fears about the U.S. plane that had strayed over Soviet territory at a time when American military forces were on a high alert. They raced against the clock, wrestling with all these questions as the missiles in Cuba moved closer and closer to full operational readiness. The one point on which there was both clarity and agreement was the need for an immediate cessation of work on the missile sites.

During the morning Ex Comm meeting in which the topic is an impending show-down near the quarantine line—President Kennedy is handed a newswire report:[87]

JFK: [reading from news ticker copy handed him by Special Counsel Ted Sorensen] "Premier Khrushchev told President Kennedy yesterday he would withdraw offensive weapons from Cuba if the United States withdrew its rockets from Turkey."

BUNDY: Hmm. He didn't. . . .

JFK: That wasn't in the letter [dated October 26] we received, was it?

THEODORE SORENSEN: No. I read it pretty carefully. It doesn't read that way to me either. . . .

JFK: Well, this is unsettling now, George, because he's got us in a pretty good spot here. Because most people would regard this as not an unreasonable proposal. I'll just tell you that. In fact, in many ways—

BUNDY: But what "most people," sir—

JFK: I think you're going to have it very difficult to explain why we are going to take hostile military action in Cuba, against these sites, what we're here thinking about, when he's saying, "If you'll get yours out of Turkey, we'll get ours out of Cuba." I think you've got a very tough one here. . . . I think we have to assume that this is their new and latest position, and it's a public one. . . .

McNAMARA: . . . We had one deal in the letter; now we've got a different deal. . . How can we negotiate with somebody who changes his deal before we even get a chance to reply, and announces publicly the deal before we receive it? . . .

JFK: . . . Emotionally, people will think this is a rather even trade and we ought to take advantage of it. . . .

Later that afternoon, at the 4 p.m. meeting, the Ex Comm continues its discussion over Khrushchev's latest proposal:

LLEWELLYN THOMPSON: Mr. President, if we go on the basis of a trade, which I gather is somewhat in your mind, we end up, it seems to me, with the Soviets still in Cuba though, with planes and technicians and so on, even though the missiles are out. And that would surely be unacceptable and put you in a worse position.

JFK: Yeah, but our technicians and planes and guarantees would still exist for Turkey. I'm just thinking about what we're going to have to do in a day or so, which is 500 sorties, and seven days, and possibly an invasion, all because we wouldn't take missiles out of Turkey. We all know how quickly everybody's courage goes when the blood starts to flow. . . Today it sounds great to reject [the trade deal], but it's not going to, after we do something. . . .

I think what we've got to do is say that we've got to make the key of this letter [to Khrushchev] the cessation of work. That we're all in agreement on. There's no question about that. Then the question is whether Turkey's in or just Cuba. . . .

So I think we ought to make that the key question—the cessation of work. Then if we get the cessation of work, we can settle the Cuban question and we can do the other things. Otherwise he can hang us up for three days while he goes on with the work.

[Drafting message to Khrushchev] "The first ingredient, let me emphasize, for any solution is a cessation of the work and inoperability of the missiles under reasonable standards."

I mean I want to just come back to that. Otherwise time ticks away on us.

Shortly after 4 p.m. the Ex Comm gets word that a missing U-2 plane had been shot down over Cuba.[88]

McNAMARA: The U-2 was shot down. The fire against our low-altitude surveillance.

JFK: A U-2 was shot down?

McNAMARA: [DIA official, Col. John] Wright just said it was found shot down.

ROBERT KENNEDY: Was the pilot killed?

TAYLOR: This was shot down over Banes, which is right near a U-2 site in eastern Cuba.

UNIDENTIFIED: A SAM site.

TAYLOR: The pilot's body is in the plane. Apparently, this was a SAM site that had actually had the Fruitcake radar. It all ties in a very plausible manner.

JFK: Well now, this is much of an escalation by them, isn't it? . . .

McNAMARA: How do we interpret this? I don't know how to interpret it?. . .

JFK: How can we send a U-2 fellow over there tomorrow unless we take out all the SAM sites? . . .

PAUL NITZE: They've fired the first shot.

The meetings last throughout the afternoon. When JFK leaves the room at approximately 6:15 p.m., the discussions continue.[89]

VICE PRESIDENT LYNDON B. JOHNSON: . . . You just ask yourself what made the greatest impression on you today, whether it was his letter last night, or whether it was his letter this morning, or whether it was that U-2 boy going down.

DOUGLAS DILLON: The U-2 boy.

LBJ: That's exactly right; that's what did it. That's when everybody started to change, and that [attacking a SAM site] is what's going to make an impression on him . . .

**Wreckage of Major Anderson's
plane, not dated**

© Bettman/Corbis/AP Images

WHAT THEY DIDN'T KNOW

Khrushchev's Decision-Making Process

The U.S. response to the missile sites—President Kennedy's October 22 message to the nation and the military mobilization—alarmed the Soviets. In a gross miscalculation, Khrushchev had assumed that the United States would tolerate the presence of the missiles in Cuba. On Thursday, October 25, the Soviet Union decided to seek a diplomatic way out of the crisis—they would remove the missile sites in Cuba. On Friday, October 26, having read intelligence reports about an imminent U.S. invasion of Cuba, Khrushchev dictated his long message to President Kennedy offering to remove the missiles in exchange for a U.S. pledge not to invade Cuba. The message was conveyed through official diplomatic channels in a process that took nearly 12 hours.

Soon after, Khrushchev began to have second thoughts. He did not believe that President Kennedy would resort to force. As the Soviet leader's son, Sergei Khrushchev, later recalled: "Father decided to try to change horses in midstream . . . now it was all logical: the [U.S.] base in Turkey in exchange for the [Soviet] base in Cuba."[90] Quickly, Khrushchev dictated another letter demanding removal of the Jupiter missiles in Turkey. Aware of the lag time in official diplomatic channels, he ordered the letter be read over the air by Radio Moscow. It was broadcast as the Ex Comm was deliberating his original proposal.[91]

Nikita S. Khrushchev at United Nations General Assembly, September 1, 1960

Photograph by Art Rickerby

© *Time Life Pictures/ Getty Images*

The View from Cuba

In Cuba, the U.S. reconnaissance overflights were believed to be a prelude to an all-out invasion. A local government official later recalled, "During each overflight we had to assume we would be killed, that the bombing would begin, that we would never see our families again."[92]

After President Kennedy's October 22 address to the nation, Castro was convinced that a U.S. attack was imminent—that it would lead to a nuclear exchange in which Cuba would be annihilated. On the night of October 26, he wrote a message to Khrushchev that the Soviet leader understood to be a request to launch a pre-emptive nuclear strike against the United States. Castro later stated that he was only trying to boost Khrushchev's morale—to assure him of the resolve of the Cuban people.[93]

When Castro heard over the radio that Khrushchev had negotiated a resolution of the crisis with the United States on October 27, without consulting or informing the Cuban government, he was furious.[94] Castro viewed it as nothing less than the Soviet Union's betrayal of the Cuban Revolution.[95]

Republic Square, Havana, Cuba, showing the building with a giant mural of Fidel Castro and former Soviet Premier Vladimir Lenin, March 1962

Photograph by Rolls Press/ Popperfoto

© Popperfoto/Getty Images

The President Responds to Khrushchev's Messages

Khrushchev's "knot of war" letter of October 26 proposed a deal in which the Soviets would dismantle the Cuban sites if the United States would pledge not to invade Cuba and to lift the quarantine.

Before the Ex Comm could compose a response, a different proposal came in over the newswires: *Premier Khrushchev told President Kennedy yesterday he would withdraw offensive weapons from Cuba if the U.S. withdrew its rockets from Turkey.*

Against the counsel of nearly all his advisers, the President saw in this second proposal a way out of the crisis, and insisted on giving it every possible consideration. Ultimately, the United States responded to Khrushchev's proposals in two parts: the first part was President Kennedy's written message to Premier Khrushchev. It was drafted and approved by the Ex Comm early in the evening of October 27 and reached the State Department at 8:05 p.m.

The second part of the message was conveyed orally when Attorney General Robert Kennedy personally handed the letter to Soviet Ambassador Dobrynin at 7:45 that evening.

In the end, JFK offered the Kremlin a calculated blend of Khrushchev's October 26 and October 27 proposals:

- the removal of the Soviet missiles from Cuba.
- an American non-invasion pledge.
- a willingness to talk later about NATO-related issues.
- a secret commitment to withdraw the Jupiter missiles from Turkey.[96]

President Kennedy's response to Premier Khrushchev's proposal, essentially agreeing to the Premier's earlier proposal, October 27, 1962

" You would agree to remove these weapons systems from Cuba. . . . We, on our part, would agree . . . to remove the quarantine measures now in effect and . . . to give assurances against an invasion of Cuba.

. . . the first ingredient, let me emphasize, is the cessation of work on missiles sites in Cuba. "

John F. Kennedy Presidential Library and Museum, Boston, Massachusetts

second letter which you made public. I would like to say again that the United States is very much interested in reducing tensions and halting the arms race; and if your letter signifies that you are prepared to discuss a detente affecting NATO and the Warsaw Pact, we are quite prepared to consider with our allies any useful proposals.

But the first ingredient, let me emphasize, is the cessation of work on missile sites in Cuba and measures to render such weapons inoperable, under effective inter-national guarantees. The continuation of this threat, or a prolonging of this discussion concerning Cuba by linking these problems

Secret Agreement Regarding U.S. Missiles in Turkey, October 27, 1962

Unbeknownst to at least half of the Ex Comm, President Kennedy authorized Attorney General Robert Kennedy to convey a willingness on the part of the United States to remove the missiles in Turkey, if pressed on the matter—but that part of the agreement would have to remain secret.

Shortly after taking office in 1961, President Kennedy had expressed an interest in removing the missiles in Turkey; they were all but obsolete. But there was concern that doing so under pressure of the current crisis could be interpreted as a betrayal of the U.S. alliance with the Turks.

After the meeting, Robert Kennedy returned to the White House and later recalled the President's mood and expectations: "The president was not optimistic. . . . He ordered 24 troop-carrier squadrons of the Air Force Reserve to active duty. They would be necessary for an invasion. . . . The expectation was a military confrontation by Tuesday and possibly tomorrow."[97]

Memorandum for the Secretary of State from the Attorney General, describing his October 27 meeting with Ambassador Dobrynin, October 30, 1962, page 3

This memo is Robert Kennedy's account of the historic encounter.

The sentence on page 3 that has a line drawn through it relates to the removal of the missiles in Turkey. There is no evidence to tell us by whom or for what purpose it was crossed out. But it may well reflect the administration's concern for secrecy on this question. Robert Kennedy was instructed to warn Dobrynin that any disclosure of the secret agreement would render it null and void.[98]

" He then asked me about Khrushchev's other proposal dealing with the removal of the missiles from Turkey. I replied that there could be no quid pro quo—no deal of this kind could be made. . . . If some time elapsed . . . I mentioned 4 or 5 months—I said I was sure that these matters could be resolved satisfactorily. "

John F. Kennedy Presidential Library and Museum, Boston, Massachusetts

> Memorandum for
> The Secretary of State   October 30, 1962
>
> He asked me then what offer we were making. I said a letter had just been transmitted to the Soviet Embassy which stated in substance that the missile bases should be dismantled and all offensive weapons should be removed from Cuba. In return, if Cuba and Castro and the Communists ended their subversive activities in other Central and Latin-American countries, we would agree to keep peace in the Caribbean and not permit an invasion from American soil.
>
> He then asked me about Khrushchev's other proposal dealing with the removal of the missiles from Turkey. I replied that there could be no quid pro quo -- no deal of this kind could be made. This was a matter that had to be considered by NATO and that it was up to NATO to make the decision. I said it was completely impossible for NATO to take such a step under the present threatening position of the Soviet Union. ~~If some time elapsed -- and per your instructions, I mentioned four or five months -- I said I was sure that these matters could be resolved satisfactorily.~~
>
> Per your instructions I repeated that there could be no deal of any kind and that any steps toward easing tensions in other parts of the world largely depended on the Soviet Union . . .

STEPPING BACK FROM THE BRINK

Remove them. As quickly as possible. Before something terrible happens.

Nikita S. Khrushchev, October 28, 1962 [99]

The final and most critical stages of these negotiations between Kennedy and Khrushchev took place on the open airwaves, simply because it was the fastest means of communication.[100] With the world on the edge of nuclear war, speed trumped secrecy.

On Sunday, October 28, Khrushchev and his advisers assembled at a dacha outside Moscow. With events escalating, the Soviet Premier was anxious to end the crisis as soon as possible; he started to dictate a letter to President Kennedy informing him that the missile sites in Cuba would be removed.[101] When Khrushchev learned that the United States had made a secret offer to remove its missiles from Turkey, he readily agreed to keep that part of the agreement secret.[102] To end the crisis as soon as possible, couriers rushed Khrushchev's message to the Moscow radio station, where it was broadcast around the world at approximately 4 p.m., 9 a.m. in Washington.[103]

Dismantling of the sites in Cuba began at 5 p.m. that afternoon.[104]

Portion of Khrushchev's message to the President, broadcast by Radio Moscow, October 28, 1962

The Soviet government has ordered the dismantling of bases and the dispatch of equipment to the USSR. ... I wish to again state that the Soviet government has offered Cuba only defensive weapons. I appreciate your assurance that the United States will not invade Cuba. Hence we have ordered our officers to stop building bases, dismantle the equipment, and send it back home. This can be done under U.N. supervision.

John F. Kennedy Presidential Library and Museum, Boston, Massachusetts

FBIS 47

KHRUSHCHEV MESSAGE

FOR YOUR INFORMATION L

MOSCOW DOMESTIC SERVICE IN RUSSIAN AT 1404 GMT ON 28 OCTOBER BROADCASTS A KHRUSHCHEV MESSAGE TO KENNEDY. HE DECLARES: I RECE VED YOUR MESSAGE OF 27 OCTOBER AND I AM GRATEFUL FOR YOUR APPRECIAT ON OF THE RESPONSIBILITY YOU BEAR FOR WORLD PEACE AND SECURITY.

THE SOVIET GOVERNMENT HAS ORDERED THE DISMANTLING OF BASES AND THE DISPATCH OF EQUIPMENT TO THE USSR. A FEW DAYS AGO, HAVANA WAS SHELLED, ALLEGEDLY BY CUBAN EMIGRES. YET SOMEONE MUST HAVE ARMED THEM FOR THIS PURPOSE. EVEN A BRITISH CARGO SHIP WAS SHELLED. CUBANS WANT TO BE MASTERS OF THEIR COUNTRY. THE THREAT OF INVASION HAS UPSET THE CUBAN PEOPLE.

I WISH TO AGAIN STATE THAT THE SOVIET GOVERNMENT HAS OFFERED CUBA ONLY DEFENSIVE WEAPONS. I APPRECIATE YOUR ASSURANCE THAT THE UNITED STATES WILL NOT INVADE CUBA. HENCE WE HAVE ORDERED OUR OFFICERS TO STOP BUILDING BASES, DISMANTLE THE EQUIPMENT, AND SEND IT BACK HOME. THIS CAN BE DONE UNDER U.N. SUPERVISION.

WE MUST NOT ALLOW THE SITUATION TO DETERIORATE, (BUT) ELIMINATE HOTBEDS OF TENSION, AND WE MUST SEE TO IT THAT NO OTHER CONFLICTS OCCUR WHICH MIGHT LEAD TO A WORLD NUCLEAR WAR.

WE ARE READY TO CONTINUE TO EXCHANGE VIEWS ON RELATIONS BETWEEN NATO AND THE WARSAW BLOC, DISARMAMENT, AND OTHER ISSUES OF PEACE AND WAR.

(MORE)

UNCLASSIFIED
Classification

Mr. Chairman, both of our countries have great unfinished tasks and I know that your people as well as those of the United States can ask for nothing better than to pursue them free from the fear of war. Modern science and technology have given us the possibility of making labor fruitful beyond anything that could have been dreamed of a few decades ago.

I agree with you that we must devote urgent attention to the problem of disarmament, as it relates to the whole world and also to critical areas. Perhaps now, as we step back from danger, we can together make real progress in this vital field. I think we should give priority to questions relating to the proliferation of nuclear weapons, on earth and in outer space, and to the great effort for a nuclear test ban. But we should also work hard to see if wider measures of disarmament can be agreed and put into operation at an early date. The United States Government will be prepared to discuss these questions urgently, and in a constructive spirit, at Geneva or elsewhere.

/s/ John F. Kennedy

End Text

Telegram of President Kennedy's message to Premier Khrushchev, October 28, 1962, received by the State Department and released to the press at 5:03 p.m., page 3

President Kennedy learned of Khrushchev's decision to remove the missiles from Cuba when it was broadcast on the American airwaves.

At an Ex Comm meeting later that morning, the President warned against any appearance of gloating or claiming victory.[105] In his official response, he welcomed Khrushchev's latest message as "an important contribution to peace," and stressed the importance of the two nations working together toward disarmament.

" . . . as we step back from danger . . . I think we should give priority to questions relating to the proliferation of nuclear weapons, on earth, and in outer space, and to the great effort for a nuclear test ban. "

MRBM Launch Site 1, Sagua La Grande, November 1, 1962

John F. Kennedy Presidential Library and Museum, Boston, Massachusetts [PX66-20-26]

Although the most acute phase of the confrontation ended that Sunday, the United States Strategic Air Command remained at DEFCON-2, and the quarantine remained in effect through November 20, when there was an agreement that all "offensive weapons" would be returned to the Soviet Union.

A GIFT FROM THE PRESIDENT

At the end of October, President Kennedy decided to present a memento to each of his advisers who assisted him through the ordeal. His secretary later recalled, "the one thing that was fixed in his mind was the idea of having the month of October . . . with the dates 16–28 either circled or standing out in different print."[106]

He commissioned Tiffany & Company to create 34 silver-and-wood calendar paperweights. In addition to those who participated in the Ex Comm meetings during the most intense phase of the crisis, Jacqueline Kennedy and the President's personal secretary, Evelyn Lincoln, were among the recipients.

Mrs. Kennedy and the children, Caroline and John Jr., were at a family retreat in Middleburg, Virginia, when the crisis began to unfold at the White House on October 16. Mrs. Kennedy and the children returned immediately to Washington, as the President asked, and she later remembered telling him that she wanted to remain with him at the White House, no matter what:

I said, please don't send me to Camp David. . . . If anything happens we're all going to stay here with you . . . even if there's not room in the bomb shelter in the White House . . . I said, please, then I just want to be on the lawn when it happens. . . . I just want to be with you and I want to die with you and the children do too, than live without out. So he said he wouldn't send me away."[107]

Left:

Jacqueline Kennedy's Cuban Missile Crisis calendar, a gift from President Kennedy, November 1962

Photograph by Joel Benjamin

Opposite:

Jacqueline Kennedy's Cuban Missile Crisis calendar on her desk in the White House family quarters

Photograph by Cecil Stoughton

John F. Kennedy Presidential Library and Museum, Boston, Massachusetts

THE LIMITED NUCLEAR TEST BAN TREATY

The treaty prohibits nuclear weapons testing in the atmosphere, in outer space, and underwater. Efforts to achieve a test ban agreement began in 1955 and extended over eight years.[108] Having come so close to nuclear war during the Cuban Missile Crisis, both President Kennedy and Premier Khrushchev actively sought to reduce tensions between the two nations in the months that followed.

The Limited Nuclear Test Ban Treaty, signed at Moscow, August 5, 1963, page 1

General Records of the U.S. Government

National Archives, Washington, DC

TREATY
banning nuclear weapon tests
in the atmosphere, in outer
space and under water

The Governments of the United States of America, the United Kingdom of Great Britain and Northern Ireland, and the Union of Soviet Socialist Republics, hereinafter referred to as the "Original Parties",

Proclaiming as their principal aim the speediest possible achievement of an agreement on general and complete disarmament under strict international control in accordance with the objectives of the United Nations which would put an end to the armaments race and eliminate the incentive to the production and testing of all kinds of weapons, including nuclear weapons,

Seeking to achieve the discontinuance of all test explosions of nuclear weapons for all time, determined to continue negotiations to this end, and desiring to put an end to the contamination of man's environment by radioactive substances,

Have agreed as follows:

Article I

1. Each of the Parties to this Treaty undertakes to prohibit, to prevent, and not to carry out any nuclear weapon test explosion, or any other nuclear explosion, at any place under its jurisdiction or control:

(a) in the atmosphere; beyond its limits, including outer space; or underwater, including territorial waters or high seas; or

The treaty was signed at Moscow on August 5, 1963, by U.S. Secretary of State Dean Rusk, Soviet Foreign Minister Andrei Gromyko, and British Foreign Secretary Lord Home. The treaty was proclaimed by President Kennedy and entered into force on October 10, 1963.

According to the special counsel of the President, "no other single accomplishment in the White House ever gave him greater satisfaction."[109]

Presidential Proclamation, October 10, 1963, signature page

General Records of the
U.S. Government
National Archives, Washington, DC

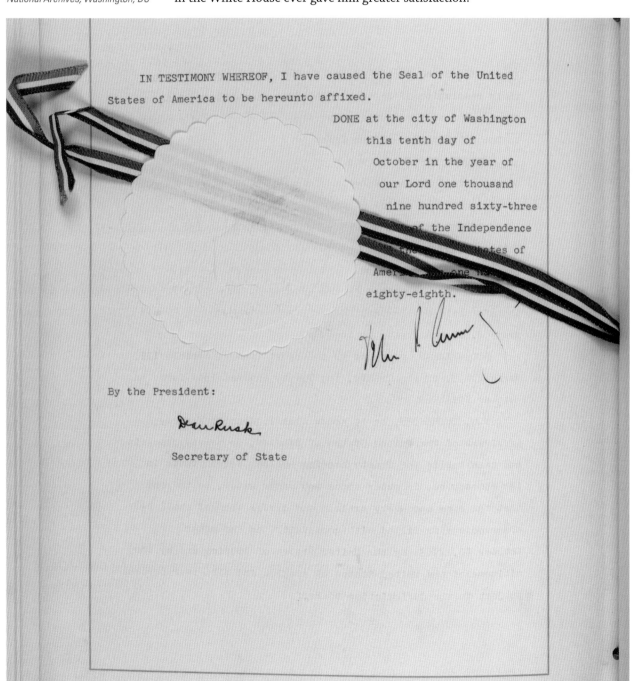

IN TESTIMONY WHEREOF, I have caused the Seal of the United States of America to be hereunto affixed.

DONE at the city of Washington this tenth day of October in the year of our Lord one thousand nine hundred sixty-three of the Independence of the United States of America the one hundred eighty-eighth.

By the President:

Dean Rusk

Secretary of State

EPILOGUE

THE LEADERS LOOK BACK

John F. Kennedy
Photograph by Fabian Bachrach

" This was an effort to materially change the balance of power, it was done in secret, steps were taken really to deceive us by every means they could, and they were planning in November to open to the world the fact that they had these missiles so close to the United States.

The real problem is the Soviet desire to expand their power and influence. . . . It is this constant determination . . . [that] they will not settle for that kind of a peaceful world, but must settle for a Communist world. That is what makes the real danger, the combination of these two systems in conflict around the world in a nuclear age is what makes the sixties so dangerous. [110] "

1962

Less than one year after the Cuban Missile Crisis, the United States and the Soviet Union reached agreement on the Limited Nuclear Test Ban Treaty.

Nikita S. Khrushchev, Moscow, U.S.S.R., April 12, 1955
© Corbis

Fidel Castro, Havana, Cuba, January 10, 1959
Photograph by Lester Cole © Lester Cole/Corbis

Actually what we were trying to achieve was to have America shake itself out of its sleep and for its leadership to get a feeling of what war actually is . . . It is a consolation to me now that on the whole we acted correctly and accomplished a great revolutionary deed. We didn't get frightened and we didn't allow American imperialism to intimidate us. So many years have passed now, and it's plain for all to see . . . that the revolutionary cause headed by Fidel Castro is still alive and flourishing. The United States made a commitment not to invade Cuba itself and not to allow its allies to invade, and thus far it has fulfilled that commitment.[111]

ca. 1969

In October 1964, Khrushchev was removed from power. His misjudgments and mishandling of the crisis over the Cuban missile sites were cited among the causes for his ouster.[112]

We started from the assumption that if there was an invasion of Cuba [by the United States], nuclear war would erupt. . . . Everybody here was simply resigned to the fate that we would be forced to pay the price, that we would disappear.

Not only were we left out from participating in seeking solutions to the crisis, but we were also left out of the historical research and the in-depth analysis of these events later on.

[W]e did have one victory, which was weapons free of charge. . . . for almost thirty years, we received our weapons and arms free from the Soviet Union. This was one of the positive aspects of the October crisis. So, we didn't want to make relations bitter. Who could profit from that? No one was going to profit from that. We simply had to control that anger.[113]

1992

Fidel Castro remained in power for 46 years after the missile crisis. He retired from official public life in 2008.

Customers in a California
department store watch
President Kennedy's televised
address to the nation, as he
informs the American people
about the unfolding crisis in
Cuba, October 22, 1962

Photograph by Ralph Crane

©Time & Life Pictures/Getty
Images

ACKNOWLEDGMENTS

It has been a privilege to work on this project marking the 50th anniversary of the Cuban Missile Crisis. The exhibition "To the Brink: JFK and the Cuban Missile Crisis" and this accompanying publication—produced jointly by the National Archives in Washington, DC, and its John F. Kennedy Presidential Library and Museum in Boston, Massachusetts—represent the efforts of many talented, dedicated professionals from both venues.

The exhibit was created with the support of the Archivist of the United States, David S. Ferriero, and under the direction of James Gardner, Executive for Legislative Archives, Presidential Libraries, and Museum Services; Susan Donius, Director, Office of Presidential Libraries; Tom Putnam, Director, John F. Kennedy Presidential Library and Museum; Marvin Pinkert, former Director of the National Archives Experience (NAE); and Christina Rudy Smith, Director of Exhibits.

It was made possible in part by the Foundation for the National Archives, the John F. Kennedy Library Foundation, and the generous support of Lead Sponsor AT&T, with special recognition to the Lawrence F. O'Brien Family.

Senior exhibit designers Ray Ruskin and Michael Jackson, NAE, Washington, DC, created the exhibit design that turned a large and complex storyline into a handsome and accessible presentation, and Rania Hassan is responsible for this book's elegant design. Benjamin Guterman edited the exhibit and book texts.

I thank the Foundation for the National Archives, under the leadership of President A'Lelia Bundles and the direction of Executive Director Thora Colot, for publishing this book. Director of Publications Patty Reinert Mason managed the project and edited the book, while Kathleen Lietzau provided editorial and administrative support. Franck Cordes, Stefanie Mathew, and Chris DerDerian also supported the publication and the exhibit through marketing, fundraising, and product development.

As always, I am grateful for the support of the John F. Kennedy Library Foundation, which, under the direction of Executive Director Tom McNaught, supports this and every exhibit project undertaken by the Kennedy Library. I also thank Ariadne Valsamis, Doris Drummond, Maura Hammer, Lee Statham, Rachel Flor, and Megan Piccirillo for supporting this project through promotion, marketing, and fundraising.

The process of selecting the documents, photographs, and audio excerpts from the White House recordings was guided by members of the Kennedy Library's archival staff under the direction of the Kennedy Library's Chief Archivist, Karen Adler Abramson. Declassification archivist Maura Porter generously shared her expertise on the Kennedy Library's Presidential Recordings at the start of this project; she also identified and located a number of key documents throughout the research and writing process. Audiovisual archivist Laurie Austin worked with us to produce the exhibit audio excerpts heard in the galleries and was an invaluable resource on the Kennedy Library's photographic holdings. Jenny Beaton, Erica Boudreau, Stacey Chandler, Maryrose Grossman, Michelle DeMartino, Paul Lydon, and Steve Plotkin also provided archival research assistance.

In Washington, archivist Michael Hussey located important CIA and State Department documents. Senior researcher Darlene McClurkin obtained a number of hard-to-find photographic images, with the assistance of Alexis Hill and Patrick Kepley from the exhibits team. Holly Reed, Theresa Roy, Nicholas Natanson, Carla Simms, and Rutha Beamon of the National Archives Still Pictures unit provided guidance in the search for images.

I am grateful to the following independent historians and scholars, not only for the body of work they have produced, but also for their assistance and guidance in helping to make the story of the crisis accurate and lively: Sheldon Stern, former historian at the Kennedy Library and author of several books about the Cuban Missile Crisis; Timothy Naftali, former director of the Presidential Recordings Program at the University of Virginia's Miller Center of Public Affairs, who also served as director of the Richard Nixon Presidential Library and Museum in Yorba Linda, California, and has authored several books and articles; and Peter Kornbluh, Director of the Cuba Documentation Project at the National Security Archives in Washington, DC. With their wealth of knowledge on the most recently released source material, they reviewed the exhibition, either in whole or in part, at various stages in its development. Michael Dobbs, author of *One Minute to Midnight: Kennedy, Khrushchev, and Castro on the Brink of Nuclear War*, shared information and illustrations produced in his work. These scholars were uniformly gracious, generous, and deft in their remarks. Their contribution cannot be overstated.

I am especially grateful to Nancy McCoy, the Kennedy Library's Director of Education and Public Programs, who early on offered thoughtful solutions to the challenge of making the story accessible to exhibit visitors. Exhibit designer Amy Forman looked at various design elements and provided helpful input.

The following museum registrars in Boston and Washington, DC, safeguarded the original documents and museum artifacts through all phases of production, managing the logistics of transporting these precious materials between Boston and Washington, and preparing them for display: Kathryn Dodge and Heather Joines, registrar and museum specialist in Boston, and Washington exhibit registrar Karen Hibbitt and senior registrar James Zeender. In Boston, museum technician Kathryn Hanson-Plass helped prepare the text for publication.

Exhibits conservator Terry Boone, from the National Archives' Conservation Division, led the conservation work on the documents and prepared them for display; she was assisted by Richard Hnat, Douglas J. McRae, and Morgan Zinsmeister.

Northern Light Productions, Boston, Massachusetts, produced the multimedia presentations that add drama and immediacy to the exhibition.

At the National Archives in Washington, DC, Tom Nastick, Public Programs producer, and Richard T. Taylor, video post production supervisor, produced the exhibit clips presenting archival footage of President Kennedy's October 22, 1962, address to the nation; Vice President Nixon's 1959 impromptu debate with Premier Khrushchev in Moscow; President Kennedy's November 2, 1961, statement on the development and testing of nuclear weapons; and an excerpt from the October 25, 1962, exchange between U.S. Ambassador Adlai Stevenson and Soviet Ambassador Valerian Zorin at the United Nations. Michelle Farnsworth, from the National Archives Digitization Services unit, created the scans used in the exhibit prints and in this publication.

Finally, I thank James Wagner, the Kennedy Library's exhibit specialist, who served as assistant curator on this project, and whose keen eye and unique sensibilities have made it a better exhibit.

"To the Brink" has been a group effort, involving colleagues in Washington and Boston. I consider myself lucky to work with them. I am grateful most of all for the wisdom, restraint, and discipline exercised by President Kennedy during those perilous days in the fall of 1962.

Stacey Bredhoff

BIBLIOGRAPHY

Blight, James G., Bruce J. Allyn, and David A. Welch. *Cuba on the Brink: Castro, the Missile Crisis, and the Soviet Collapse*. New York: Pantheon Books, 1993.

Brugioni, Dino A. *Eyeball to Eyeball: The Inside Story of the Cuban Missile Crisis*. New York: Random House, 1991.

Bundy, McGeorge. *Danger and Survival: Choices About the Bomb in the First Fifty Years*. New York: Random House, 1988.

Chang, Laurence, and Peter Kornbluh, eds. *The Cuban Missile Crisis, 1962: A National Security Archive Documents Reader*. New York: The New Press, 1998.

Dallek, Robert. *An Unfinished Life: John F. Kennedy, 1917–1963*. Boston: Little, Brown and Company, 2003.

Dobbs, Michael. "Lost in Enemy Airspace." *Vanity Fair* (June 2008).

———. *One Minute to Midnight: Kennedy, Khrushchev, and Castro on the Brink of Nuclear War*. New York: Alfred A. Knopf, 2008.

Fursenko, Aleksandr and Timothy Naftali. *Khrushchev's Cold War: The Inside Story of an American Adversary*. New York: W. W. Norton & Company, 2006.

———. *"One Hell of a Gamble": Khrushchev, Castro, and Kennedy 1958–1964*. New York: W. W. Norton & Company, 1997.

Gaddis, John Lewis. *The Cold War: A New History*. New York: Penguin Press, 2005.

———. *We Now Know: Rethinking Cold War History*. Oxford: Clarendon Press, 1997.

George Washington University. "The Cuban Missile Crisis, 1962: The Photographs." *http://www.gwu.edu/~nsarchiv/nsa/cuba_mis_cri/photos.htm* (accessed August 20, 2012).

Hansen, James H. "Soviet Deception in the Cuban Missile Crisis." Last modified June 27, 2008. *https://www.cia.gov/library/center-for-the-study-of-intelligence/csi-publications/csi-studies/studies/vol46no1/article06.html* (accessed March 15, 2012).

Isachenkov, Vladimir. "Russian Book Looks at Missile Crisis." Review of *Cuban Samba of the Foxtrot Quartet*, by Alexander Mozgovoi. Johnson's Russia List, 6320. June 21, 2002. *http://www.apnewsarchive.com/2002/Russian-Book-Looks-at-Missile-Crisis/id-90e64877cc72530d93be726668cff122* (accessed June 6, 2012).

John F. Kennedy Presidential Library. "Nuclear Test Ban Treaty." *http://www.jfklibrary.org/JFK/JFK-in-history/Nuclear-Test-Ban-Treaty.aspx* (accessed May 14, 2012).

Kennedy, Jacqueline. *Jacqueline Kennedy: Historic Conversations with John F. Kennedy, Interviews with Arthur M. Schlesinger, Jr., 1964*. Foreword by Caroline Kennedy, Introduction and annotations by Michael Beschloss. New York: Hyperion, 2011.

Kennedy, John F. Presidential Papers. John F. Kennedy Presidential Library, Boston, MA.

———. President's Office Files. John F. Kennedy Presidential Library, Boston, MA.

———. *Public Papers of the Presidents of the United States: January 20–December 31, 1961*. Washington, DC: Government Printing Office, 1962.

———. White House Audio Recordings, 1961–1963. John F. Kennedy Presidential Library, Boston, MA.

Kennedy, Robert F. *Thirteen Days: A Memoir of the Cuban Missile Crisis*. New York: W. W. Norton & Company, 1969.

Kent, Sherman. "The Cuban Missile Crisis of 1962: Presenting the Photographic Evidence Abroad." Spring 1972. *http://www.fas.org/irp/imint/cubakent.htm* (accessed May 14, 2012).

Khrushchev, Sergei, ed. *Memoirs of Nikita Khrushchev: Statesman, 1953–1964*, Vol. 3 of *Memoirs of Nikita Khrushchev*. University Park, PA: The Pennsylvania State University Press, 2007.

———. *Nikita Khrushchev and the Creation of a Superpower*. University Park, PA: The Pennsylvania State University Press, 2000.

May, Ernest R., and Philip D. Zelikow, ed. *The Kennedy Tapes: Inside the White House During the Cuban Missile Crisis*. New York: W. W. Norton & Company, 2002.

Mozgovoi, Alexander. *The Cuban Samba of the Quartet of Foxtrots: Soviet Submarines in the Caribbean Crisis of 1962*. Translated by Svetlana Savranskaya, the National Security Archive. Moscow: Military Parade, 2002.

Polmar, Norman, and John D. Gresham. *DEFCON-2: Standing on the Brink of Nuclear War During the Cuban Missile Crisis*. Hoboken, NJ: John Wiley & Sons, Inc., 2006.

Reeves, Richard. *President Kennedy: Profile of Power*. New York: Simon & Schuster, 1993.

Rusk, Dean. *As I Saw It: Dean Rusk as told to Richard Rusk*. New York: W. W. Norton & Company, 1990.

Sorensen, Theodore C. *Kennedy*. Old Saybrook, CT: Konecky & Konecky, 1965.

Stern, Sheldon M. *Averting 'The Final Failure': John F. Kennedy and the Secret Cuban Missile Crisis Meetings*. Stanford, CA: Stanford University Press, 2003.

———. *The Week the World Stood Still*. Stanford, CA: Stanford University Press, 2005.

U.S. Department of State. "Background Note: Cuba." Last modified November 7, 2011, *http://www.state.gov/outofdate/bgn/cuba/191090.htm* (accessed June 1, 2012).

———. "Treaty Banning Nuclear Weapon Tests in the Atmosphere, in Outer Space and Under Water." *http://www.state.gov/t/isn/4797.htm* (accessed July 10, 2012).

Visual Content Entertainment. "The Cuban Missile Crisis, Timeline of Events." *http://www.atomcentral.com/cuban-missile-crisis.aspx* (accessed May 10, 2012).

ENDNOTES

1   John F. Kennedy, "Address in New York City Before the General Assembly of the United Nations," September 25, 1961, in *Public Papers of the Presidents of the United States, January 20–December 31, 1961* (Washington, DC: United States Government Printing Office, 1962), 623.
2   John F. Kennedy, Television and Radio Interview: "After Two Years—a Conversation With the President, December 17, 1962," in *Public Papers of the Presidents of the United States*, 898–899
3   John Lewis Gaddis, *We Now Know: Rethinking Cold War History* (Oxford: Clarendon Press, 1997), 206–11.
4   "Background Note: Cuba," U.S. Department of State, last modified November 7, 2011, *http://www.state.gov/outofdate/bgn/cuba/191090.htm* (accessed June 1, 2012).
5   Gaddis, *We Now Know*, 206–11.
6   Sheldon Stern, email message to author, May 17, 2012, and Laurence Chang and Peter Kornbluh, eds. *The Cuban Missile Crisis, 1962: A National Security Archive Documents Reader* (New York: The New Press, 1998), xxvi–xxvii.
7   John F. Kennedy Presidential Library, "Nuclear Test Ban Treaty," *http://www.jfklibrary.org/JFK/JFK-in-history/Nuclear-Test-Ban-Treaty.aspx* (accessed May 14, 2012).
8   Richard Reeves, *President Kennedy: Profile of Power* (New York: Simon & Schuster, 1993), 175.
9   John F. Kennedy, "Address Before the American Society of Newspaper Editors," April 20, 1961, *Public Papers of the Presidents of the United States*, 305.
10 Aleksandr Fursenko and Timothy Naftali, *"One Hell of a Gamble": Khrushchev, Castro, and Kennedy 1958–1964* (New York: W. W. Norton & Company, 1997), 39–40, 362 n. 23.

11   "A Program of Covert Action against the Castro Regime," approved by President Eisenhower at a meeting in the White House on March 17, 1960, White House Office, Office of Staff Sec. International Series, Box 4, Dwight D. Eisenhower Library, quoted in Fursenko and Naftali, *"One Hell of a Gamble,"* 44, 362 n. 34.

12   Tim Naftali, email message to author, July 3, 2012.

13   Theodore C. Sorensen, *Kennedy* (Old Saybrook, CT: Konecky & Konecky, 1965), 309.

14   Fursenko and Naftali, *"One Hell of a Gamble,"* 146–48.

15   Sheldon M. Stern, *Averting 'The Final Failure': John F. Kennedy and the Secret Cuban Missile Crisis Meetings* (Stanford, CA: Stanford University Press, 2003), 15.

16   Chang and Kornbluh, eds., *A NSA Documents Reader*, 363.

17   Fursenko and Naftali, *"One Hell of a Gamble,"* 196.

18   Nikita Khrushchev, "Wars of National Liberation" (speech given at the Higher Party School of the Institute of Marxism-Leninism, Moscow, January 6, 1961), quoted in Gaddis, *We Now Know*, 183.

19   Tim Naftali, email message to author, July 3, 2012.

20   Fursenko and Naftali, *"One Hell of a Gamble,"* 171, 181.

21   Ibid., *"One Hell of a Gamble,"* 191.

22   James H. Hansen, "Soviet Deception in the Cuban Missile Crisis: Getting the Cubans On Board," last modified June 27, 2008, *https://www.cia.gov/library/center-for-the-study-of-intelligence/csi-publications/ csi-studies/studies/vol46no1/article06.html* (accessed March 15, 2012).

23   Fursenko and Naftali, *"One Hell of a Gamble,"* 205–6.

24   Ibid.

25   Robert Dallek, *An Unfinished Life: John F. Kennedy, 1917–1963* (Boston: Little, Brown and Company, 2003), 539.

26   Hansen, "Soviet Deception in the Cuban Missile Crisis."

27   Tim Naftali, email message to author, July 1, 2012.

28   Fursenko and Naftali, *"One Hell of a Gamble,"* 217.

29   Ibid., 220.

30   Ibid., 221.

31   Dino A. Brugioni, *Eyeball to Eyeball: The Inside Story of the Cuban Missile Crisis* (New York: Random House, 1991), photograph captions 13, 14.

32   Sherman Kent, "The Cuban Missile Crisis of 1962: Presenting the Photographic Evidence Abroad," Spring 1972, *http://www.fas.org/irp/imint/cubakent.htm* (accessed May 14, 2012).

33   Reeves, *President Kennedy*, 368.

34   Sorensen, *Kennedy*, 673.

35   Stern, *Averting 'The Final Failure,'* xxii.

36   Ibid., xxiii.

37   Ibid., xxii.

38   Fursenko and Naftali, *"One Hell of a Gamble,"* 217.

39   Robert F. Kennedy, *Thirteen Days: A Memoir of the Cuban Missile Crisis* (New York: W. W. Norton & Company, 1969), 24.

40   Ibid., 45.

41   Chang and Kornbluh, eds., *A NSA Documents Reader*, 126.

42   President's Office Files, Countries Series, Box 115, Cuba: Security, 1962. John F. Kennedy Presidential Library. (JFKPOF-115-004-p0006) See also Chang and Kornbluh, eds., *A NSA Documents Reader*, 129–30.

43   Chang and Kornbluh, eds., *A NSA Documents Reader*, 131.

44   Ernest R. May and Philip D. Zelikow, ed., *The Kennedy Tapes: Inside the White House During the Cuban Missile Crisis*, (New York: W. W. Norton & Company, 2002), 76.

45   Robert S. McNamara, introduction to *Thirteen Days*, by Robert F. Kennedy, 15.

46   May and Zelikow, *The Kennedy Tapes*, 90.

47 Ibid., 109.

48 Stern, *Averting 'The Final Failure'*, 122.

49 Sorensen, *Kennedy*, 696.

50 Reeves, *President Kennedy*, 387.

51 Reeves, *President Kennedy*, 392; Sorensen, *Kennedy*, 702.

52 Stern, *Averting 'The Final Failure,'* 159–61.

53 May and Zelikow, *The Kennedy Tapes*, 174.

54 James G. Blight, Bruce J. Allyn, and David A. Welch, *Cuba on the Brink: Castro, the Missile Crisis, and the Soviet Collapse* (New York: Pantheon Books, 1993), 59.

55 Michael Dobbs, *One Minute to Midnight: Kennedy, Khrushchev, and Castro on the Brink of Nuclear War* (New York: Alfred A. Knopf, 2008), 51.

56 Brugioni, *Eyeball to Eyeball,* 398, 401.

57 Dobbs, *One Minute to Midnight*, 85–86.

58 May and Zelikow, *The Kennedy Tapes*, 107. Stern, email message to author, May 17, 2012.

59 Stern, *Averting 'The Final Failure,'* 202; Reeves, *President Kennedy*, 399.

60 May and Zelikow, *The Kennedy Tapes*, 217.

61 John F. Kennedy, "Radio and Television Report to the American People on the Berlin Crisis," July 25, 1961, *Public Papers of the Presidents of the United States,* 536.

62 Dallek, *An Unfinished Life*, 466.

63 Visual Content Entertainment,"The Cuban Missile Crisis, Timeline of Events." *http://www.atomcentral. com/cuban-missile-crisis.aspx* (accessed May 9, 2012). Between October 15 and November 1, six nuclear tests took place in the Johnston island area of the Pacific Ocean.

64 May and Zelikow, *The Kennedy Tapes*, 231.

65 Stern, *Averting 'The Final Failure'*, 213–14.

66 Ibid., 208.

67 Chang and Kornbluh, eds., *A NSA Documents Reader*, 382. This exchange is not on the tapes.

68 Dobbs, *One Minute to Midnight*, 91. Rusk's "eyeball to eyeball" remark is not on the tapes.

69 Stern, *Averting 'The Final Failure,'* 244.

70 Vladimir Isachenkov, "Russian Book Looks at Missile Crisis," review of *Cuban Samba of the Foxtrot Quartet*, by Alexander Mozgovoi, Johnson's Russia List, 6320, June 21, 2002, *http://www.apnewsarchive. com/2002/Russian-Book-Looks-at-Missile-Crisis/id-90e64877cc72530d93be726668cff122* (accessed June 6, 2012).

71 Alexander Mozgovoi, *The Cuban Samba of the Quartet of Foxtrots: Soviet Submarines in the Caribbean Crisis of 1962*, trans. Svetlana Savranskaya, the National Security Archive (Moscow: Military Parade, 2002). See also Stern, *Averting 'The Final Failure,'* 214 n. 191. See also Dobbs, *One Minute to Midnight*, 301–3.

72 "The Cuban Missile Crisis, 1962: The Photographs," photo 35, *http://www.gwu.edu/~nsarchiv/nsa/ cuba_mis_cri/photos.htm* (accessed August 10, 2012).

73 Fursenko and Naftali, *"One Hell of a Gamble,"* 262.

74 Dobbs, *One Minute to Midnight*, 164.

75 Reeves, *President Kennedy*, 399.

76 Ibid.

77 Kennedy, *Thirteen Days*, 51.

78 Stern, *Averting 'The Final Failure,'* 258.

79 Dobbs, *One Minute to Midnight,* 131–32

80 Ibid., 242.

81 Norman Polmar and John D. Gresham. *DEFCON-2: Standing on the Brink of Nuclear War During the Cuban Missile Crisis* (Hoboken, NJ: John Wiley & Sons, Inc., 2006), 149–50; Sergei Khrushchev, *Nikita Khrushchev and the Creation of a Superpower* (University Park, PA: The Pennsylvania State University Press, 2000), 606–8.

82 Dobbs, *One Minute to Midnight*, 268–69.

83 Michael Dobbs, "Lost in Enemy Airspace," *Vanity Fair*, June 2008; Stern, *Averting 'The Final Failure,'* 307–8. Polmar and Gresham, *DEFCON-2*, 151–52; Khrushchev, *Nikita Khrushchev and the Creation of a Superpower*, 606–8.

84 Dobbs, "Lost in Enemy Airspace," 218.

85 Fursenko and Naftali, *"One Hell of a Gamble,"* 277–80.

86 Dobbs, *One Minute to Midnight*, 294–95.

87 Stern, *Averting 'The Final Failure,'* 291; May and Zelikow, *The Kennedy Tapes*, 303.

88 Fursenko and Naftali, *"One Hell of a Gamble,"* 280.

89 Stern, *Averting 'The Final Failure,'* 352.

90 Khrushchev, *Nikita Khrushchev and the Creation of a Superpower*, 596.

91 Aleksandr Fursenko and Timothy Naftali, *Khrushchev's Cold War: The Inside Story of an American Adversary* (New York: W. W. Norton & Company, 2006), 483–91, 616 n. 69.

92 Blight, Allyn, and Welch, *Cuba on the Brink*, 102.

93 Ibid., 251–52, 361, 481–82.

94 Ibid., 32, 214–25.

95 Fursenko and Naftali, *Khrushchev's Cold War*, 490.

96 Sheldon Stern, Notes, May 17, 2012

97 Kennedy, *Thirteen Days*, 109.

98 McGeorge Bundy, *Danger and Survival: Choices About the Bomb in the First Fifty Years.* (New York: Random House, 1988), 433; Stern, *Averting 'The Final Failure,'* 478.

99 Sheldon Stern, *The Week the World Stood Still* (Stanford, CA: Stanford University Press, 2005), 195.

100 Bundy, *Danger and Survival*, 444.

101 Dallek, *An Unfinished Life*, 570; Fursenko and Naftali, *"One Hell of a Gamble,"* 284–85; Fursenko and Naftali, *Khrushchev's Cold War*, 489–90.

102 Fursenko and Naftali, *"One Hell of a Gamble,"* 284–85; Fursenko and Naftali, *Khrushchev's Cold War*, 490.

103 Fursenko and Naftali, *"One Hell of a Gamble,"* 287.

104 Stern, *Averting 'The Final Failure,'* 384, 389.

105 Sorensen, *Kennedy,* 717.

106 Evelyn Lincoln, "Cuban Crisis Calendar," President's Office Files, Subjects Series, Box 98, Cuban Missile Crisis memento. John F. Kennedy Presidential Library. (JFKPOF-098-007-p0007)

107 Jacqueline Kennedy, *Jacqueline Kennedy: Historic Conversations on Life with John F. Kennedy, Interviews with Arthur M. Schlesinger, Jr., 1964.* Foreword by Caroline Kennedy, Introduction and annotations by Michael Beschloss (New York: Hyperion, 2011), 263.

108 U.S. Department of State, "Treaty Banning Nuclear Weapon Tests in the Atmosphere, in Outer Space and Under Water," *http://state.gov/t/isn/4797.htm* (accessed Jul 11, 2012).

109 Sorensen, *Kennedy*, 740.

110 John F. Kennedy, Television and Radio Interview: "After Two Years—a Conversation With the President." December 17, 1962, *Public Papers of the Presidents of the United States*, 897–98.

111 Sergei Khrushchev, ed., *Memoirs of Nikita Khrushchev: Statesman, 1953–1964,* Vol.3 (University Park PA: The Pennsylvania State University Press, 2007), 339–40.

112 Fursenko and Naftali, *"One Hell of a Gamble,"* 353–54.

113 Blight, Allyn, and Welch, *Cuba on the Brink,* 251, 32, 366.